CRITIC
THE WORK

The Last to Fall

"Authors Jim Rada and Richard Fulton have done an outstanding job of researching and chronicling this little-known story of those Marines in 1922, marking it as a significant moment in Marine Corps history."

- *GySgt. Thomas Williams*
Executive Director
U.S. Marine Corps Historical Company

"Original, unique, profusely illustrated throughout, exceptionally well researched, informed, informative, and a bit iconoclastic, "The Last to Fall: The 1922 March, Battles, & Deaths of U.S. Marines at Gettysburg" will prove to be of enormous interest to military buffs and historians."

- *Small Press Bookwatch*

Saving Shallmar

"But Saving Shallmar's Christmas story is a tale of compassion and charity, and the will to help fellow human beings not only survive, but also be ready to spring into action when a new opportunity presents itself. Bittersweet yet heartwarming, Saving Shallmar is a wonderful Christmas season story for readers of all ages and backgrounds, highly recommended."

- *Small Press Bookwatch*

Battlefield Angels

"Rada describes women religious who selflessly performed life-saving work in often miserable conditions and thereby gained the admiration and respect of countless contemporaries. In so doing, Rada offers an appealing narrative and an entry point into the wealth of sources kept by the sisters."

- *Catholic News Service*

Between Rail and River

"The book is an enjoyable, clean family read, with characters young and old for a broad-based appeal to both teens and adults. Between Rail and River also provides a unique, regional appeal, as it teaches about a particular group of people, ordinary working 'canawlers' in a story that goes beyond the usual coverage of life during the Civil War."

- *Historical Fiction Review*

Canawlers

"A powerful, thoughtful and fascinating historical novel, Canawlers documents author James Rada, Jr. as a writer of considerable and deftly expressed storytelling talent."

- *Midwest Book Review*

"James Rada, of Cumberland, has written a historical novel for high-schoolers and adults, which relates the adventures, hardships and ultimate tragedy of a family of boaters on the C&O Canal. ... The tale moves quickly and should hold the attention of readers looking for an imaginative adventure set on the canal at a critical time in history."

- *Along the Towpath*

October Mourning

"This is a very good, and very easy to read, novel about a famous, yet unknown, bit of 20th Century American history. While reading this book, in your mind, replace all mentions of 'Spanish Flu' with 'bird flu.' Hmmm."

- *Reviewer's Bookwatch*

SECRETS OF THE
GETTYSBURG BATTLEFIELD

Little-Known Stories & Hidden History
From the Civil War Battlefield

Other books by James Rada, Jr.

Non-Fiction
- Battlefield Angels: The Daughters of Charity Work as Civil War Nurses
- Beyond the Battlefield: Stories from Gettysburg's Rich History
- Clay Soldiers: One Marine's Story of War, Art, & Atomic Energy
- Echoes of War Drums: The Civil War in Mountain Maryland
- The Last to Fall: The 1922 March, Battles & Deaths of U.S. Marines at Gettysburg
- Looking Back: True Stories of Mountain Maryland
- Looking Back II: More True Stories of Mountain Maryland
- No North, No South: The Grand Reunion at the 50th Anniversary of the Battle of Gettysburg
- Saving Shallmar: Christmas Spirit in a Coal Town

Secrets Series
- Secrets of the C&O Canal: Little-Known Stories & Hidden History Along the Potomac River
- Secrets of Catoctin Mountain: Little-Known Stories & Hidden History Along Catoctin Mountain
- Secrets of Garrett County: Little-Known Stories & Hidden History of Maryland's Westernmost County

Fiction
- Between Rail and River
- Canawlers
- Lock Ready
- October Mourning
- The Rain Man
- Smoldering Betrayal

SECRETS OF THE
GETTYSBURG BATTLEFIELD

Little-Known Stories & Hidden History
From the Civil War Battlefield

Dick, how many secrets do you know?

by
James Rada, Jr.

LEGACY
PUBLISHING

A division of AIM Publishing Group

SECRETS OF THE GETTYSBURG BATTLEFIELD: LITTLE-KNOWN STORIES AND HIDDEN HISTORY FROM THE CIVIL WAR BATTLEFIELD

Published by Legacy Publishing, a division of AIM Publishing Group. Gettysburg, Pennsylvania.
Printed in the United States of America.
First printing: February 2019.

ISBN 978-0-9998114-9-8

Some of the articles in this collection have previously appeared in the *Gettysburg Times, Celebrate Gettysburg,* and *The Gettysburg Companion.* Sometimes where additional information is available the stories have been updated.

Cover design by Grace Eyler.

LEGACY
PUBLISHING

315 Oak Lane • Gettysburg, Pennsylvania 17325

For Ben Rada.
He's not around much anymore,
but his family still loves him

CONTENTS

What Happened at Gettysburg?

For many historians, the Battle of Gettysburg was the turning point of the Civil War. It was the most massive battle of the Civil War with 165,620 Union and Confederate troops fighting over July 1-3, 1863.

Confederate Gen. Robert E. Lee brought the Army of Northern Virginia north of the Potomac River for the second time during the war. He wanted to scare northern politicians by reaching a large city, such as Harrisburg, Pa., or Philadelphia, Pa. His hope that seeing a city in danger would encourage them to seek a truce. Lee also wanted to relieve northern Virginia, which the war had ravaged.

Lee moved north in May 1863 with Union Gen. Joseph Hooker and the Army of the Potomac pursuing. Maj. Gen. George G. Meade assumed command of the army on June 28.

The two armies met at Gettysburg, Pa., in a chance encounter on July 1. Gettysburg was a small town where 11 roads converged, but it became the site of a major battle as both armies reinforced their lines outside of the town. With the battle engaged, Lee sought another win, this one on Union soil.

Union Brig. Gen. John Buford defended the ridges northwest of the town with cavalry and two corps of infantry. Two corps of Confederate infantry attacked Buford and his men from the north and northwest and overwhelmed them.

The Union lines collapsed, and the soldiers retreated through Gettysburg to the south of the town.

In a scene from the Gettysburg Cyclorama, Gen. Alexander Webb leads the Union attack from atop his white horse. Courtesy of the National Park Service.

On July 2, the Union lines assembled along the hills to the south of town. The defensive formation resembled a fishhook. Gen. Lee launched his assault against the left flank of the Union army. Heavy fighting took place at Little Round Top, Devil's Den, the Wheatfield, and the Peach Orchard. The Confederates also attacked the Union lines on the right at Culp's Hill and Cemetery Hill.

At the end of the day, the Union lines still held, but the number of casualties was climbing on both sides.

The fighting continued for a third day. In one final act to break the Union lines, 12,500 Confederate infantry charged the center of the Union line on Cemetery Ridge. Known as Pickett's Charge, the Confederate soldiers took heavy losses against the Union artillery and rifles and did not break through the line.

The Confederate Army finally retreated into Maryland, then crossed the Potomac River and back into Virginia.

It was a costly battle on both sides. Of the 51,112 casualties, 23,049 were Union soldiers (3,155 killed, 14,529 wounded, and 5,365 missing and captured) and 28,063 were Confederate soldiers (3,903 killed, 18,735 wounded, and 5,425 missing and captured).

In a scene pictured in the Gettysburg Cyclorama, Arnold's Battery A 1st Rhode Island Light Artillery fires into the charging Confederate soldiers. Courtesy of the National Park Service.

The Union victory encouraged, rather than discouraged, the north to continue fighting. The battle also led to one of the greatest speeches in history. President Abraham Lincoln traveled to Gettysburg on Nov. 19 to take part in the dedication of the Soldiers National Cemetery. His short speech honoring the dead soldiers and laying out the purpose for the war is now known as the Gettysburg Address.

THE BATTLE OF GETTYSBURG

Confederates Burn the Home of Stonewall Jackson's Uncle

T he threat of invasion loomed heavy over Gettysburg on July 1, 1863. Many people had fled the area to be out of the way of flying bullets and artillery shells.

On the bluff overlooking Willoughby Run, west of Gettysburg, sat the "Old McLean Place," a colonial mansion where Rev. Charles McLean lived. McLean, the pastor of the Gettysburg Presbyterian Church, was also the uncle of Confederate Gen. Stonewall Jackson.

The residents of the McLean Mansion decided to remain in their home "for ours was of the old-fashioned fortress type with 18 inch walls and heavy wooden shutters. My aunt and I, then but a school girl, were quite alone, our farmer having gone away with the horses in the hope of hiding them in the fastness of the hills," wrote Amelia Harman, a young girl who attended the Oakridge Seminary on Chambersburg Pike.

They heard cannon booming to the west around 9 a.m.

"We rushed to the window to behold hundreds of galloping horses coming up the road, through the fields and even past our very door. Boom! Again spoke the cannon, more and more galloping horses, their excited riders shouting and yelling to each other and pushing westward in hot haste, past the house and the barn, seeking the shelter of a strip of woods on the ridge beyond," Harman wrote.

Gen. Thomas Jonathan "Stonewall" Jackson

Soldiers hid behind the barn, outbuildings, trees, and even the water pump while those people in the house probably wondered whether 18-inch thick walls were thick enough.

"Filled with alarm and terror we locked all the doors and rushed to the second floor - and threw open the shutters of the west window. Once glance only and a half-spent Minnie (sic) ball from the woods crashed into the shutter close to my aunt's ear leaving but the thickness of paper between her and death," Harman wrote.

Before getting away from the window, they had seen Confederate soldiers hidden in the tall grass shooting any Union soldier who appeared.

Amelia and her aunt saw an officer beneath their window whose horse was shot out from under him.

"Look, the field is full of Rebels," they shouted to the man.

"Leave the window or you'll be killed!" the officer

warned them.

Harman and her aunt climbed into the cupola of the mansion that offered an even more-expansive view of the countryside. "It seemed as though the fields and woods had been sown with dragon's teeth, for everywhere had sprung up armed men, where but an hour ago only grass and flowers grew," Amelia wrote.

They witnessed the Rebels leave the cover of the forest a quarter mile away to engage the Union soldiers in a battle that killed Union Gen. John Reynolds.

Meanwhile, the Union soldiers decided they wanted to take cover within the house. They pounded on the door to be let inside and took up positions at the windows. The women retreated to the cellar.

They had poor views from below the ground. However, they could hear "roar of heavy musketry, galloping horses, yelling troops and the occasional boom of cannon to the westward."

"The suspense and agony of uncertainty were awful! We could hear the beating of our own hearts above all the wild confusion. How long this lasted I know not. Of a sudden there came a scurrying of quick feet, a loud clattering on the stairway above, a slamming of doors and then for an instant – silence!" Harman wrote.

Then they heard marching and saw the lower legs of soldiers who were wearing Confederate gray. The women realized that the Union soldiers had retreated.

Harman and her aunt ventured up to the first floor and saw that the barn was in flames and Rebels soldiers in the house were setting it afire. Later reports said Confederate soldiers burned the house to deprive the Union sharpshooters their hiding place.

"We burned it very reluctantly, but it was the only way

we could get them out," Captain Little of the 52nd North Carolina wrote after the battle.

"They had taken down a pile of newspapers for kindling, piled on books, rugs and furniture, applied matches to ignite the pile, and already a tiny flame was curling upward. We both jumped on the fire in hope of extinguishing it, and pleaded with them in pity to spare our home. But there was no pity in those determined faces. They proceeded to carry out their full purpose and told us to get out or we would burn with it," Harman wrote.

The women had no choice but to flee outside where there was still fighting going on.

"We were between the lines! To go toward town would be to walk into the jaws of death. Only one way was open - through the ranks of the whole Confederate army to safety in its rear!" Harman wrote.

They ran in that direction. As they did, they saw soldiers fall as others urged them to the rear of the fighting. They walked around two miles before they came upon a group of officers and reporters talking in the shelter of trees.

A reporter from the *London Times* not only listened to their story but led them further away to a cottage where he assured them they would be safe. The reporter then reported the situation to Confederate Gen. Robert E. Lee, who promised to station a guard around the cottage.

"We were doubtless the only persons on the Union side who were fed from Gen. Lee's commissary during the Battle of Gettysburg. And so far as I know, our house was the only one actually set on fire deliberately by the enemy," Harman wrote.

When they were able to return to their four days later, they found only a blackened ruin where their beautiful home had stood.

As He Died, His Thoughts Were of His Secret Wife

I n the late 1800s, an old woman died in Illinois. She was the last one in her family, which only became known when she died, and no living relatives could be found. What also became known was just how sad a life the woman had lived.

The woman's mother was long dead, and her brother and father had been killed in the Civil War. Her sister had died years earlier, leaving behind an orphaned baby. The woman took care of her nephew, loving him as if he was her own child.

"She was a very sad, old-young looking woman and seemed to worship the little boy baby," the *Chicago Tribune* reported.

The woman rented a small store and went into the millinery business to support herself and the child. Despite her caring attention, her nephew died from diphtheria when he was only 15 years old.

She died five years later.

When officials went through the woman's things, they found a letter written to the woman that she had saved in a trunk. It was written on a scrap of paper, but she had cared for over the years.

A soldier, identified in the letter only as Robert, was

wounded during the Battle of Gettysburg and lay in one of the many hospital sites dying after the battle. However, he took some of the precious few minutes left of this life to write to the old woman, then a young woman in the prime of her life. Robert never wrote her name, but he addressed the letter to Mrs. O. E. W. of Corliss, Wisconsin.

Camp Letterman was one of the battlefield hospital sites established after the Battle of Gettysburg. Photo courtesy of the Library of Congress.

The letter begins with something that came as a surprise to anyone who had known the old woman. Everyone believed she had been an "old maid," but the letter quickly vanquished that idea.

"Oh! little girl, I did so great a wrong to you when I coaxed you to marry me secretly. I am so far from you and I was so careless in not seeing to it that you received a wedding certificate," Robert began.

She could not get one because Robert wrote that the minister who had married them had died, and he must not have recorded the marriage.

Robert wrote of being heartsick and longing to be with his wife and regretting the short time they had spent together.

He closes the letter, but then added a postscript later. The postscript notes that it was written after the battle.

"All hope is gone. I am lying here and the nurse tells me the doctor says there is no hope for me. I wanted to be with you so badly, and now I can't even see you at the last. Remember that I loved you and would have given my whole life to make you happy. I pray God to help you and to forgive me my sin toward you, but oh! I loved you so," he wrote.

Robert then told his wife he was growing weaker and the nurses were telling him he needed to stop and rest. He lamented that he would never again see his wife again. His final words are oddly chilling. "Good-by. It is getting dark."

The couple has never been identified beyond the clues in the letter. Since Robert addressed the woman as Mrs. O. E. W., we can assume that Robert's last name began with W and that he was probably from Wisconsin since that is where his wife was living. However, 2,135 men from Wisconsin fought in the battle of Gettysburg, and more than one Robert W. fell.

The marriage of Robert and his wife not only remained a mystery during their lives, it remains a mystery to this day.

Confederate Army Takes Civilian Prisoners After the Battle of Gettysburg

I n March of 1865, the country was still at war, but the end was near. The Confederacy was collapsing, and the Union was pressing its advantage and forcing the Confederate Army to retreat.

They weren't surrendering easily, though. Just a couple weeks earlier, 40 McNeill's Rangers had snuck into Union-occupied Cumberland, Md., and kidnapped Gen. George Crook and Gen. Benjamin Kelley from their hotel rooms. The Rangers escaped back into Virginia and delivered the prisoners to the infamous Libby Prison where the Confederate Government ransomed them back to the Union Government.

The generals' incarceration hadn't even lasted a month. They were lucky.

Around the same time negotiations were underway to free the generals, several men returned home to Adams County. They had been missing for 20 months. They weren't victorious soldiers. They were farmers, postmasters, and ordinary citizens. They were also a secret, or perhaps, a shame of the Confederacy because these men were civilians whom the Army arrested at the end of the Battle of Gettysburg. They were marched back to Virginia as prisoners when the Confederate

Army retreated.

"The hostages were selected from three target groups. They were agents of the government such as postmasters or tax collectors, they defied or criticized the invaders or they were prominent citizens in the community," James Cole, a descendant of one hostage, said in a 1994 interview.

On July 2, 1863, Confederate soldiers arrested Samuel Pitzer and his uncle, George Patterson, on the suspicion that they were spies.

Rebel sharpshooters hidden behind the Pitzer Schoolhouse surprised Pitzer and Patterson. The two men argued they were farmers not spies. The soldiers told them they would have to go to the headquarters for a hearing.

"As they did not find any firearms upon us they assured us that we would not be held after the hearing. When we reached headquarters however Major Fairfax said it was too late to give the hearing that night and put if off till morning," Pitzer wrote of his experiences years later and reported in the *History of the St. James Lutheran Church*.

The following day, the Union Army prevailed and the Confederate Army started its retreat. The soldiers forgot about holding a hearing, and the prisoners were forced to march south, accompanied by a guard who stood beside each prisoner.

Emanuel Trostle, was another Gettysburg farmer. He lived with his wife and child on Emmittsburg Road. During the battle, a Confederate colonel rode up to his farmhouse and warned him that his family was in danger because of the battle.

"Mr. Trostle, who was crippled at the time, and walked with the aid of a staff and crutch, told the colonel that he could not pass through his pickets. The colonel told him that he would take him through, and accordingly did so," the *Gettysburg Times* reported in 1914 when Trostle died.

Trostle had second thoughts the next morning, though. He worried about some of the household goods he had left behind and headed back, accompanied by a friend. They got as far as the pickets before Confederate soldiers captured them.

"He was taken to the battle-field, expecting to be paroled, but the firing opened before the parole could be made out. He was taken to Staunton, Va., walking the entire distance of 175 miles; was on the road six days, and for three days had not a mouthful to eat," according to the *Gettysburg Times*.

Civilians Endure Horrors of POW Camps

When the Confederate Army left Pennsylvania at the end of the Battle of Gettysburg, they left with eight civilians. These men had done nothing wrong except be in the wrong place at the wrong time. They were captured at different locations around Gettysburg on the suspicion that they were spies for the Union Army.

They weren't.

They were ordinary citizens caught in the middle of a great battle.

The arrested men were George Codori, J. Crawford Guinn, Alexander Harper, William Harper, Samuel Pitzer, George Patterson, George Arendt, and Emanuel Trostle.

Confederates arrested Gettysburg farmer Samuel Pitzer on July 2. He wrote that the prisoners were first sent to Castle Lightning prison in Richmond where all of their money except for two cents, their knives, and their blankets were taken.

They were then moved to Libby Prison. This upset Pitzer because someone there stole his hat, which he said would have been worth $150 to $200 in Confederate dollars.

"The first thing we hear when new prisoners came in was

'Fresh Fish,' to which another would immediately reply 'Scale him,' and it was not long they had them all scaled," Pitzer wrote.

The rations were poor, so much so that even the pigs ate better.

"They raise beans down there on which they fatten their hogs," Pitzer wrote. "We got a broth with about a dozen of these beans and a little corn bread."

Some of the civilians arrested after the Battle of Gettysburg were held in Libby Prison in Richmond as POWs. Photo courtesy of Wikimedia Commons.

After a time, they were sent to Castle Thunder Prison where the rations were even worse.

The commander there was a Union army deserter named George Edwards. He had a reputation for brutality. Pitzer wrote that he would make the prisoners stand around him while he swung his sword back and forth coming close to slicing the prisoners open.

After two months in Richmond, the prisoners were sent further south to Salisbury, N.C., where they were imprisoned in an old tobacco factory. At first, there were 500 prisoners in the factory prison, but during October 1863, that number swelled to 14,000.

BIRD'S EYE VIEW OF CONFEDERATE PRISON PEN
AT SALISBURY, N.C. ——— TAKEN IN 1864

The Confederate Army took Gettysburg residents and held them in the Confederate prison in Salisbury, N.C. Courtesy of Wikimedia Commons.

What little food the prisoners received left a lot to be desired. In the beginning, their rations consisted of a little meat that was "strong and so full of worm holes we could see through it," according to Pitzer.

Other days, the guards simply threw a little beef and tripe into the garrison and let the prisoners fight over who got to eat it.

Sometimes the prisoners weren't fed for two or three days at a time. It was a tactic used to encourage them to join the Confederate army so they could be used to guard forts and camps.

The prisoners got to where they were eating just about anything they thought would fill them up.

"They ate rats, cats and dogs and I saw an Irishman eating the graybacks as he picked them from his clothes," Pitzer wrote.

Within four months the 14,000 prisoners dwindled in number to 4,500 as men died from malnutrition.

"As regularly as the day returned from forty to sixty died," Pitzer wrote.

The dead were buried in a common grave four bodies deep.

The Gettysburg civilians endured, though, not knowing when the end would come, but knowing it would come eventually.

Civilian POWs Return Home

"Both Pennsylvania and the U. S. government informed the Confederacy that they had taken noncombatant civilians, and demanded their return. Because it refused, and since it was regarded as an act of state terrorism, the U. S. Secretary of War ordered the U. S. Army to seize 26 Confederate civilians and hold them as counter hostages at the Fort Delaware Prison on the Delaware River," according to the *Gettysburg Times*.

The fort is on Pea Patch Island in the Delaware River between Delaware and New Jersey. It had granite and brick walls that ranged in thickness from seven to 30 feet and were 32 feet high. Conditions for prisoners there were unpleasant, although not as unpleasant as things had been in Salisbury Prison for the Gettysburg civilian prisoners.

One Union doctor wrote of his visit to the prison. It is included in *The War Of The Rebellion: A Compilation Of The Official Records Of The Union And Confederate Armies.* "The barracks were at that time damp and not comfortably warm, and I suspect they have been so a part of the time during the winter...Some, perhaps a large majority, were comfortably clad. Some had a moderate and still others an insufficient supply of clothing. The garments of a few were ragged and filthy. Each man had one blanket, but I observed no other bedding nor straw. Nearly all the men show a marked neglect of personal cleanliness. Some of them seem vigorous and well, many look only moderately well, while a considerable number have an unhealthy, a cachectic appearance."

In early 1865, the Gettysburg civilian POWs finally got their hearing before Gen. John H. Winder in Richmond. "He called some of us disloyal Pennsylvanians. I told him I was loyal to the backbone," Samuel Pitzer wrote after the war.

This led to their release and they returned home to Gettysburg in the middle of March 1865.

The returning prisoners surprised many because their families presumed most of the civilian prisoners dead after the battle. Emanuel Trostle's wife hadn't given up hope that her husband still lived. Her dedication was rewarded when he returned home. He went on to lead a successful life as a shoemaker and a farmer.

He died in 1914 at the age of 75. He lived to see the 50th anniversary of the Battle of Gettysburg and perhaps, the same men who had captured him during the battle. It is not known whether he attended the reunion, though.

George Codori's return on March 13 got a small mention in the *Adams Sentinel*. The joy of his return lasted only two weeks. He died of pneumonia at the age of 59.

"For a number of years he had had an attack of this dangerous disease almost every winter, but during the past 18 months, though suffering the privations incident to the life of a prisoner of the South, he informed us his health was very good," the *Gettysburg Compiler* reported. It is believed he caught a cold riding the crowded transport that brought freed prisoners to Annapolis and dropped them off.

Ironically, three days after Codori died, the Pennsylvania House of Representatives and Senate released a joint resolution asking "That the Secretary of War be respectfully requested to use his utmost official exertions to secure the release of J. Crawford Gwinn, Alexander Harper, George Codori, William Harper, Samuel Sitzer (sic), George Patterson, George Arendt, and Emanuel Trostle, and such other civilians, citizens of Pennsylvania, as may now be in the hands of the rebels authorities, from rebel imprisonment and have them returned to their respective homes in Pennsylvania."

Lincoln's Chair Vanishes

On November 19, 1863, thousands of people gathered in Gettysburg for the dedication of Soldiers' National Cemetery. The keynote speaker of the event was Edward Everett. As his speech continued on and on, people standing in the crowd had to sit or risk their legs buckling. On the stage, the speakers had chairs to rest on until their time to speak came.

President Abraham Lincoln sat in a rocking chair between Everett and Secretary of State William Seward.

"Mr. Lincoln sat on the platform all the time in a rude, little stiff-backed chair, hard, and uncomfortable, but he hardly ever moved," Dr. Henry Jacobs recalled in the *Gettysburg Times* in 1923. He had been a young boy in the audience at the dedication.

When Everett finished his two-hour speech, the president stood up from his rocker, walked to the podium and delivered 286 words we still recall today as one of the great speeches of American history.

Today, you can see the chair that President Abraham Lincoln was sitting in when John Wilkes Booth shot him. You can see the chair he sat in while writing portions of his Gettysburg Address, but whatever happened to the rocking chair Lincoln sat on during the dedication ceremony?

That's a tricky question.

Gettysburg College owns it...maybe.

In 1847, Gettysburg College (then Pennsylvania College) students built Linnaean Hall, primarily as a place to display their rock and mineral collections. Over the years, other collections were placed on display in the hall. At first, the scientific collections featured shells, plants and animals. Then they became historical.

"Miscellaneous collections included coins, Indian relics; natural curiosities, battlefield memorials, and the like. A few stray items such as an ivory cane used by Abraham Lincoln, and a paper signed by George Washington, have also been found," The *Gettysburgian* reported in 1937.

One of those "stray" items was an armless, cane-backed rocking chair that is supposed to have been the one that Lincoln sat upon during the dedication ceremony for Soldiers' National Cemetery. The problem is no record exists as to where the chair came from. The records may have been lost, damaged, or never existed at all. In its early days, the college did not have the controls it does now.

This can be seen in the fact that Linnaean Hall had no security for its collections. "The building was open to visitors at all times, and as a result people finally began to steal the valuable collections," *The Gettysburgian* reported in 1937.

The Lincoln chair was apparently a victim of such a theft. When it disappeared from Linnaean Hall in the early 1920's, "No public ado" was made of it, according to the *Gettysburg Times* in 1945.

"College officials knew the chair had disappeared but there was nothing to indicate its whereabouts—and little reason to hope that it might ever be recovered," the *Gettysburg Times* reported.

Linnaean Hall was demolished in 1942 and what remained of the exhibits was moved to the east end of the third floor of Glatfelter Hall, at least the collections that were still around.

"Since there was no place to store the large rock and mineral collections, and geology was taught no longer, they were hauled to a local dump and deposited. As a footnote to this travesty, the October 1, 1942 issue of the *Gettysburg Times* would note that 'The accumulation of junk has been removed, the pigeons and squirrels have found new abodes, the students have no more windows to smash, the Owl and Nightingale Club has no place for its sign, and Joe the Janitor has several hundred square feet more lawn to mow,'" Jay Lininger wrote in his article "Chronicles of Central Pennsylvania Mineralogy" on Pennminerals.com in 1998.

A part of the college's history had been lost, but as the saying goes, "History repeats itself." So it would be with Gettysburg College.

Interior view of Linnaean Hall where the Lincoln chair was originally displayed. Photo courtesy of Musselman Library Special Collections and Archives.

Lincoln's Chair Reappears

On April 7, 1945, the *Gettysburg Times* reported, "The little old rocking chair that Abraham Lincoln is reputed to have used on the platform in the National cemetery November 19, 1863, when he delivered his deathless Gettysburg Address, has come back to the sanctuary of the college campus after an absence of close to a quarter century."

The reappearance of the chair is as mysterious as its disappearance and original appearance at the college.

In March, Dr. Henry W. A. Hanson, president of Gettysburg College, received an anonymous letter from Charleston, W. Va., that alerted him that the chair was in Charleston and being offered for sale as a historical object.

The college's lawyer, Richard A. Brown, wrote back to a resident of the city and received a reply from someone who admitted that they had possession of the chair and offered to return it to the college.

"A few days after the letter was received, the carefully wrapped and crated cane-seated rocker arrived at Mr. Brown's office. From there it was sent to the college campus," the *Gettysburg Times* reported.

Who had the chair, how it made its way to West Virginia, and the price it would have fetched on the market remain unknown today. Librarians with Special Collections staff have looked through the papers of the college's past presidents seeking some clue, but have so far found nothing to authenticate the chair.

So the rocking chair with its damaged cane seat and back and scratched wood sits on a wire frame in the college archives. A yellow ribbon is draped from the back to the seat to keep anyone else from sitting on it and a small card is taped to the back of it that reads, "This chair was reputedly used by President Lincoln during the dedicatory services of the Gettysburg National Military Cemetery." This card, which has been on the chair since the college took possession, is the only record that the college has of the chair.

The chair Abraham Lincoln is believed to have sat in during the dedication of Soldiers National Cemetery.

The college did not display the chair during the 150th anniversary of the Gettysburg Address.

"We currently have the rocker in storage in Special Collections and not on public display at this time. Without documentation, it would not be fair to display it since we cannot be certain of its provenance. There is plenty more research to be done," said Carolyn Sautter, director of special collections and college archives at Gettysburg College.

The chair is protected in the college's modern archive storage built in 2001. The Special Collections staff also continues to search out more information hoping they will be able prove that not only is the chair the college currently owns the one that disappeared in the 1920's but that it is also the one that Lincoln used in 1863.

If the chair is ever authenticated, it will then be prepared for display such as removing the card and preparing a plaque describing it. Until then, it remains in a historical limbo.

Edward Woodward: Poet, Gunsmith, Souvenir Maker

dward Woodward was a creative man who came to America from England in the mid-1850s seeking an opportunity to display his creativity. What he found when he and his father arrived in Baltimore, Md., was a land of simmering tensions that soon erupted into the Civil War.

On April 19, 1861, a regiment of Massachusetts soldiers transferred between railroad stations in Baltimore. To do this they had to disembark one train and march through a city filled with Confederate sympathizers to another station where they could board a train to Washington.

The sympathizers attacked the soldiers, blocking the route and throwing bricks and cobblestones at the Union men. The soldiers panicked and fired into the mob, which led to a wild fight involving the soldiers, mob, and Baltimore police. When the fighting ended, four soldiers and 12 civilians had been killed. These deaths are considered the first of the Civil War.

Woodward was living in the city, and although it is uncertain whether he saw the melee or heard about it secondhand, it affected him.

He was a gunsmith by trade and associates who were Southern sympathizers encouraged him to go South where he would be appointed as the superintendent of a gun manufacturing plant.

His reply was, "I will never go against the flag that waved

over me when I crossed the boundless sea to this land of liberty—on it there is no rampant lion to devour nor unicorn to gore. Oh may that flag forever wave until time shall be no more," according to some of Woodward's papers still with his family.

At 47 years old, Woodward was not an ideal recruit as a soldier even though he knew his way around a rifle. Instead, he joined the Union Relief Association and cared for sick and wounded soldiers. He visited hospitals and fed sick and wounded soldiers as he spoke with them.

When the federal government took over Point Lookout, Md., and turned it into a large hospital for Union soldiers and a prisoner-of-war camp for Confederate soldiers in 1862, Woodward volunteered to help. However, his time there was cut short when he was severely wounded. Though his injury and how he received it is not known, it was severe enough he had to return home to recover.

Once Woodward recovered, he still wanted to help care for the soldiers. According to family papers, he "volunteered to go to the battlefield of Gettysburg, which he did and remained, until the closing of the hospitals, never making any charge or receiving any pay for his services." He came to Gettysburg as a member of the Christian and Sanitary Commissions, but when they moved on, he stayed behind to continue helping the sick, but to also start a new life.

He soon resumed his work as a gunsmith in the town. However, he also started a cottage industry in creating souvenirs from the relics of the battle. Woodward created desk sets that contained pieces of artillery shells and weapons. He also made engraved belt buckles from pieces of artillery shells. Some of these items sell for thousands of dollars today.

His obituary in the *Star and Sentinel* notes, "He was a man of considerable ability, and was known to nearly every student of Pennsylvania College within 25 years."

Meanwhile, the Homestead Orphanage opened in 1866 to national fanfare. There was much to admire about the operation at first, but then Rosa Carmichael was hired in 1870 as the orphanage matron. Things soon changed and rumors spread that Carmichael mistreated the children under her care.

Edward Woodward used relics from the Gettysburg Battlefield to create souvenirs that are now considered collector's items. Photo courtesy of Antiquesnavigator.com

A story about two of the orphans, Bella Hunter and Lizzie Hutchison was one of the early warning signs. When the two girls tore their dresses, Carmichael made them wear boys' clothing for two months. This seemed to be the tip of the iceberg as other stories came out.

"All sorts of stories were told," Mark H. Dunkelman wrote in *Gettysburg's Unknown Soldier*. "Mrs. Carmichael was said to have suspended children by their arms in barrels. She had hidden mistreated victims from the prying eyes of inspectors. Most scandalous of all were tales of a dungeon in the Homestead cellar, a black hole eight feet long, five feet deep, and only four feet high, unlit and unventilated, where she shackled children to the wall."

It was also noticed that the orphans could no longer decorate the soldiers' graves in Soldier's National Cemetery on Memorial Day. It all finally became too much for Woodward who had cared for some of those dead soldiers during their last days.

He expressed his anger in a broadside called "Poem" that he then distributed throughout town. The poem criticized Carmichael's treatment of Bella and Lizzie, calling her "a modern Borgia" and wrote of the orphans, "They are kept like galley slaves, while strangers decorate their father's graves."

He wrote two other poems that have survived. One is titled "Woman's Sin was a Blessing." It talks about how Eve should be viewed as a good and gentle woman and not simply as the one who brought about the Fall.

The other poem is called "What Did the Soldiers Endure" and deals with Woodward's wartime work in hospitals. It reads in part:

"They left their homes surrounded with every pleasure,
To defend the flag, their country's greatest treasure;
The native born American, and the volunteer exile,
Marched to the battlefields in rand and file—
"How cheerfully they marched, no fear, wounded they fell,
Devoted to the flag they admired and loved so well.
On the street you see a man with an empty coat sleeve
And another on crutches, oh! how it makes us grieve."

Edward Woodward died on January, 28, 1894, at age 79. Although he had been in ill health for years, the end came quickly. He fell sick on a Wednesday and died on Sunday from "inflammation of the bowels," according to the *Star and Sentinel*. He is buried in Evergreen Cemetery in Gettysburg.

Hanover Reporter on Gettysburg Address Gets Her Recognition

M ary Shaw Leader of Hanover got up early on November 19, 1863, and started off on her walk to work. Hours later, after a cold 15-mile walk, she arrived in Gettysburg to attend the dedication of the Soldiers' National Cemetery. Since the Battle of Gettysburg in July, the cemetery had been laid out and the remains of the soldiers killed in the battle had been reinterred.

She, along with hundreds of other people, stood through U.S. statesman Edward Everett's two-hour-long speech and President Abraham Lincoln's less-than-three-minute speech.

Eyewitness accounts of Lincoln's speech, which would become known as "The Gettysburg Address", say the initial reaction to it was mixed. Historian Shelby Foote said applause was "barely polite." Sarah Cooke Myers, who attended the speech, recalled in 1931, "There was no applause when he stopped speaking." However, the *New York Times* article on the speech said Lincoln was interrupted five times by applause.

When Leader returned to Hanover, she prepared her article for the *Hanover Spectator*, a newspaper owned by her family. Her father, Senary Leader, had started the newspaper in 1844, publishing it until he died in1858. Senary's wife, Maria, took over as editor while Leader served as a reporter. She was one of Pennsylvania's first female reporters.

Leader began her article, "On Thursday last, the 19th of November, 1863, was a great day in the history of Pennsylvania and the entire Union. The battlefield of Gettysburg was dedicated with imposing ceremonies in honor of the great victory which decided of the fate of the Nation."

She included the full text of Lincoln's speech and called it a "remarkable speech." Although the country was still engaged in war and would be for two more year, her view of the Battle of Gettysburg turned out to be prophetic as the battle is seen by many as the turning point of the Civil War.

Mary Shaw Leader

Leader "was the only contemporary newswriter to praise what many consider was the greatest speech ever delivered in the English language," the *Gettysburg Times* reported.

While other newspapers (usually Republican) praised the speech, it's uncertain how many of those newspapers had reporters at Gettysburg to hear it firsthand.

The Leader home in Hanover, Pa., also served as the office of the Hanover Spectator office in the addition on the left. Photo courtesy of theunfinishedwork.com

Leader passed away in Hanover in 1913 while 15 miles away Gettysburg was celebrating the largest gathering of Civil War veterans ever during the 50th anniversary of the Battle of Gettysburg.

She was buried in Mt. Olivet Cemetery with a small marker.

William Anthony, a job printer in Hanover, learned his trade from the Leader family. After Leader's death, Anthony discovered her small place in history and felt that it should be recognized with more than a small stone. He began a campaign to raise money for a larger memorial that cost $402 (about $9,500 today).

Anthony also arranged a memorial dedication service patterned after the cemetery dedication services in 1863. Around 600 people attended the service on November 10, 1941. Gettysburg College history professor, Dr. Robert Fortenbaugh, delivered the dedication address. Rev. Dr. Harry Hursh Beidleman, pastor at St. Matthew's Lutheran Church in Hanover, read the Gettysburg Address. The Reformed Emmanuel Church a cappella choir sang a Civil War song and 15-year-old Wirt Crapster, Leader's grand-nephew unveiled the monument.

MONUMENTS & VISITORS

40

Refighting the
Battle of Gettysburg

T wenty-seven years after the North and South fought
Battle of Gettysburg, it had to be fought again. This
time the battlefield was in the courts.

The 72nd Regiment Pennsylvania Volunteers, commanded by Col. DeWitt Clinton Baxter helped the Union
beat back Pickett's Charge on July 3, 1963. The regiment also known as Baxter's Fire Zouaves numbered 458 men on
the morning of July 3. The regiment held a supporting position at the rear of the Union line on Cemetery Ridge. In the
heat of the battle, the regiment moved forward to take part in
fighting back Pickett's Charge and lost 192 men or 42 percent of its soldiers.

In 1887, the Commonwealth of Pennsylvania appropriated $125,000 to pay for monuments on the Gettysburg Battle-
field to remember the state units that had fought there. According to the Pennsylvania Memorial, 34,530 Pennsylvanians fought at Gettysburg in 69 regiments of infantry, nine
regiments of cavalry, and seven batteries of artillery.

Many units, including the 72nd Pennsylvania, already had
monuments on the battlefield that had been paid for with private donations. "By this time, the 72nd had a monument on
Cemetery Ridge, but regiments that had already erected a
private monument on the battlefield could receive $1,500 for

a second state-funded one, with positions to be determined by five state commissioners working in tandem with five representatives from each regiment," Tom Huntington wrote in "A Monumental Lie: The Statue at 'Bloody Angle'."

Members of the 72nd Pennsylvania gather for a reunion in Gettysburg. Photo courtesy of Wikimedia Commons.

The following year, survivors of the 72nd Pennsylvania Infantry, with the support of the state-appointed commissioners, came before the Gettysburg Battlefield Memorial Association and asked permission to place its state-funded monument much closer to the stone wall.

Pennsylvania created the GBMA "to hold and preserve, the battle-grounds of Gettysburg." In doing so, the state also gave the association the authority to determine where to place any memorials on the Gettysburg Battlefield.

The authority of the GBMA and state-appointed commissioners came into conflict because the GBMA did not approve the location the regiment and state-appointed commissioners had agreed upon. The association's policy was to place regimental monuments where each unit was when it entered the fighting. For the 72nd Pennsylvania Infantry, this was much further back from the stone wall.

Things then became murky as records and memories of veterans, officials, state commissioners, and the GBMA differed as to what was agreed upon and with what stipulations. Veterans took sides about where the monument should be located. In this instance, however, instead of the North fighting the South, it was Union units fighting with each other.

"The survivors even purchased land in front of the wall, where they could erect their monument if necessary," Huntington wrote.

And it looked like it would be necessary as the GBMA refused to change its policy for a single regiment.

Finally, the 72nd took action. Capt. John Reed, chairman of the 72nd Pennsylvania Monument Commission, started a crew laying the foundation for the new monument on the land the regiment owned in December 1888. The GBMA saw this as trespassing and ordered Reed arrested even though he was on land the 72nd Pennsylvania owned.

The GBMA issued a statement at the time of the arrest saying, "if every regiment should be allowed to place its memorial wherever it desired there would be nothing historically correct about marking the positions of the various commands, and more monuments would be located on Seminary Ridge, in the midst of the Confederate lines, than on the Union line," according *to The Philadelphia Record.*

Getting nowhere, the 72nd Pennsylvania Infantry decided that it was time to take their case to court.

The regiment sued the Gettysburg Battlefield Memorial Association in January 1889. David Wills, representing the

GBMA, challenged the suit and had it dismissed. Refusing to surrender, the regiment took the case to the Pennsylvania Supreme Court. The court sided with the regiment and returned the case to the county court.

William A. McClean was appointed the master who heard both sides of the case on Oct. 3-4, 1890. One critical point in the testimony was an admission by the counsel for the GBMA. "It is admitted that the 72nd Regiment fought in line on the position indicated by testimony of Maj. Samuel Roberts and advanced fighting down to the stone wall, having men killed and wounded in the advance," according to the *Gettysburg Star and Sentinel.*

The lawyers later tried to withdraw this admission, but McClean would not allow it. This meant that testimony from soldiers that would have supported the 72nd Pennsylvania's location during the fighting being closer to where the GBMA wanted the monument was excluded. Col. J. B. Bachelder, who had spent much of his career mapping out where the fighting took place during the battle, could not testify because he wasn't considered an expert in the matter in the legal sense of the word because he hadn't taken part in the battle.

McClean ruled that the GBMA did not have the authority to overrule the state commissioners on placing the monuments. The GBMA appealed the decision to the state supreme court, which then rejected the appeal.

Pennsylvania Supreme Court Justice Sterrett wrote, "… the Commonwealth, acting through the agency of the commission, has the right to designate the position where any of her regiments specially distinguished themselves."

The minutes of the GBMA reflect the bitterness that the organization felt at the decision: "This, in view of the manifest unfairness and weakness of the Master's findings, was a surprise to many. It was perhaps unfortunate for our Association that the Master, in the case, would have been the son of the Presiding Judge. The opinion of the Court seems to give evidence of the resentment felt at the sharp criticism of counsel on the Master because of his unfair and illogical findings."

The 72nd Pennsylvania Zouave Memorial. Author photo.

The new monument with a Zouave swinging his rifle like a club to portray the intensity of the fighting was dedicated on July 4, 1891, twenty feet behind the stone wall. The monument's engraving reads: "During Cannonading Which Preceded the Charge the Regiment was in Line 60 Yards to the Left and Rear of This Monument When the Rebels Forced the Troops from the First Line the 72nd Fought its Way to the Front and Occupied the Wall."

About 1,000 people attended the dedication, and Edward McPherson accepted the monument on behalf of the GBMA.

While the GBMA accepted the monument, it did not accept its position on the battlefield. The organization's minutes note, "This mislocation of the 72nd monument is the only break in the harmony of the entire field. It is the only act done for which we feel that an apology is required to be made to any one. In so locating it, law was misunderstood and misinterpreted; facts were misunderstood, and inferences were unjustifiably drawn."

Although not everyone was happy with the decision, the 72nd Pennsylvania's decision to buy a tract of land for the monument helped keep the Gettysburg Electric Railway from building a trolley across the field of Pickett's Charge. The regiment refused to grant the trolley company a right-of-way to pass through the regiment's land.

Despite surviving the legal storms, the monument could not stand against Mother Nature. On June 25, 2013, less than a week before the 150th anniversary of the battle, high winds topped the 1,500-pound Fire Zouave sculpture off its pedestal. National Park Service personnel hoisted the sculpture back in place the next day.

A Visit from French Royalty

P rince Philippe, Comte de Paris, may have been French royalty and a pretender to the French throne, but he was a genuine Union veteran of the Civil War treated like royalty when he traveled in the United States.

Philippe and his brother, Prince Robert, Duke of Chartres, joined the Union Army in September 1861. Philippe was appointed as a captain and served on Maj. Gen. George McClellan's staff for nine months. He also wrote what many consider to be a one of the greatest reference books about the Civil War that there is.

When the rumor circulated through Pennsylvania College that the count would visit the Gettysburg battlefield in 1890, the students were eager to meet him. On the day he was supposed to arrive, students rushed from their classrooms when they heard the October 14 afternoon train pulling into the station, only to find out he wouldn't be arriving until the evening.

Disappointed, they returned to their classes, but when the train carrying the Count pulled into the station at 6 p.m., a crowd of students were there to greet him.

The *Pennsylvania College Spectrum* reported that the students came up with their own cheer, "Comte de Paris – Rah! Rah! Rah! – Siss, boom, tiger, Penn-syl-va-ni-yah."
The Count stepped out onto the platform before the crowd and thanked them for their hearty reception and told them he was thrilled to be in Gettysburg.

The Count of Paris, his party, and guests, during their tour of the Gettysburg. Courtesy of the Adams County Historical Society.

He spent the evening as a guest at David Wills' home and the following morning, he began a tour of the battlefield accompanied by "more corps commanders, tha[n] participated in the battle, than have been together at any time since the close of the civil war," the *Pennsylvania College Monthly* reported.

The Civil War corps commanders included: John Newton, commander of the 1st Corps; Abner Doubleday, commander of the 1st Corps; Dan Sickles, commander of the 3rd Corps; Dan Butterfield, commander of the 5th Corps; Horatio G. Wright, commander of the 6th Corps; Oliver Howard, commander of the Eleventh Corps; Henry Slocum, commander of the Twelfth Corps; and John Gregg, commander of the Cavalry Corps.

The group of generals, guests, and the Count rode around the battlefield with different generals riding with the Count in his carriage at different times to present their memorials about what had happened on the battlefield 22 years earlier.

The tour began at the Lutheran Theological Seminary, including a visit to the cupola. From there, they traveled to the site of General Reynolds' death, then along Reynolds Avenue to Mummasburg Road to Barlow's Knoll. They then returned to town for breakfast.

After breakfast, the tour resumed at Soldiers National Cemetery, then onto Culp's Hill and to the Peach Orchard. This last location was where Gen. Sickles had disobeyed orders during the Battle of Gettysburg and, depending whom you speak to, saved Union soldiers' lives or cost the Union the position.

At one point, Gen. Howard walked up to the Count of Paris and Gen. Sickles and said, "I am convinced, General, the more I look at the subject, that your movement was the proper one with plenty of troops, and saved Little Round Top by gaining time and checking rebels," the *Star and Sentinel* reported.

The group then visited Devil's Den, the Wheat Field, and Little Round Top. They followed Hancock Avenue to the Bloody Angle, and from there to Meade's Headquarters on Taneytown Road, and finally, the cavalry field.

During the tour, the Count was given a cane made from a tree near where Gen. Hancock had been wounded. "On it were pen and ink sketches of Devil's Den, the Count, Gens. McClellan and Meade, and Meade's Headquarters," the *Star and Sentinel* reported.

That evening, a reception was held for the Count in Brua Chapel on the Pennsylvania College Campus. The students who had welcomed the Count at the railroad station showed up early at the chapel to get the best seats in the house. The corps commanders, along with generals John Gobin and Orland Smith, Pennsylvania College President Harvey McKnight, and other guests joined the Count on the stage. Wills gave the opening address while Sickles served as the master of ceremonies.

When the Count spoke to the group, he said, in part, "I shall not be presumptuous enough to make a speech in this sanctuary, where I have come to accomplish a double purpose, a pilgrimage to the shrine of the noble martyrs of military duty, and a study of some of the most interesting problems of historical science. If this study has been made under such favorable circumstances, I owe it to the kind assistance of those who surround me tonight," according to the *Pennsylvania College Monthly*. A *Gettysburg Times* article in 1949 noted that the Count's accent was so heavy "no one could understand his English."

The magazine noted that the speeches made that evening were "unexceptional," but "Throughout he was spoken of as the Christian gentleman, historian and soldier, who had faced the dangers of war with us in our darkest days and thus had shown himself a friend in the time of sore trial."

After the Count returned to France, he sent a large autographed photo, which Wills had requested, to him as a thank you for the hospitality he had received in Gettysburg.

Making Peace at Gettysburg

A fter the Civil War ended, it still took time for the wounds to heal. Not so much the physical wounds but spiritual ones. The Gettysburg Battlefield was one of those wounds. Those soldiers who survived the battle had lost friends and comrades during the fighting. Some of them weren't willing to forgive and forget.

But as they say, "Time heals all wounds," and so it was with Gettysburg.

Maj. William McKendree Robbins was a native of North Carolina, but he had fought in the Civil War with the 4th Alabama Infantry. His unit had fought at Gettysburg, and Robbins had been one of those survivors who lost friends to Union bullets. He was also wounded at the Wilderness along the Plank Road.

He had moved on with his life after the war. He was elected to the U.S. Congress in 1873, and he spent three terms representing North Carolina helping govern the state he had fought against.

In 1894, President Grover Cleveland appointed him to serve on the Gettysburg Battlefield Commission as the southern commissioner. Robbins had also been a strong proponent of reconciliation between the North and the South after the war, but not everyone was as supportive.

A year later, Robbins joined in the dedication of the 32nd Massachusetts Memorial as "a silent participant," he wrote in his journal.

The 32nd Massachusetts Infantry had withstood a Confederate attack on July 2, 1863, east of Emmitsburg Road on the present-day Sickles Road. The unit had also fought later at the Wheatfield. All together, 79 out of the 227 officers and men were killed or wounded.

William M. Robbins

The monument is a six-foot tall representation of a tent with a canteen hanging from the tent pole. The regiment's information concerning the Battle of Gettysburg is inscribed on the side of the tent.

Robbins wrote that he attended "as seemed to be my official duty as a Commissioner. I joined in singing the patriotic songs. The veterans present were quite as friendly to me as if we had fought on the same side in the Civil War and I felt quite at ease among them."

Not only had he been able to reconcile his feelings from the war, but so had the survivors of the 32nd Massachusetts. Not everyone felt that way.

Later in the day, Robbins rode over the battlefield with some of the survivors of the 32nd Massachusetts. As they talked, the Union veterans admitted that a minister in their group apparently did not have the spirit of forgiveness in him.

The Massachusetts men told Robbins that when the minister had learned that Robbins was a Confederate veteran, he said, "What does that rebel mean by making himself so free and familiar among us today?"

One veteran quickly replied, "Well, I guess he thinks the war is over."

"We all had a good laugh together over the lingering prejudice of the preacher, the only man there who felt so," Robbins wrote.

This small incident showed that the healing from the war had begun, though there was still work to do.

Robbins remained on the commission until his death in 1905 and he did his part to help make sure that the Confederate story at Gettysburg was told.

"It was Robbins dream that the Confederates would memorialize the battlefield in much the way that their Union opponents had, but for a variety of reasons that never came to pass. On the battlefield today there is only one iron tablet dedicated to a Confederate regiment: that of the 4th Alabama on South Confederate Avenue, designed and paid for by Robbins," according to the website, Draw the Sword's article, "Important People in the History of the Park."

Teddy Roosevelt's Second Visit to Gettysburg

W hen Theodore Roosevelt first visited Gettysburg in 1904, he was President of the United States. Citizens welcomed him with great enthusiasm. However, he didn't run for re-election in 1908, and his chosen successor Howard Taft won election. Soon after the election, however, Taft and his policies fell out of favor with Roosevelt to the point where Roosevelt ran against his former Secretary of War in the 1912 Presidential election.

In February 1912, it was announced that Roosevelt would once again visit Gettysburg to speak during the Memorial Day ceremonies. Before that, he would also speak at a luncheon in a large tent that would be erected near the Bloody Angle where 2,000 people could gather.

The invitation to speak on Memorial Day came from the National Brotherhood of Locomotive Engineers (NBLE), which would be holding a conference in Harrisburg at the same time.

Roosevelt arrived in Gettysburg at 10 a.m. on May 30, 1912. Judge Swope, Dr. T.C. Billheimer, NBLE's Grand Chief Warren Stone and I.J. Mosey met Roosevelt at the Western Maryland train station. Despite the excitement that surrounded his first visit, Roosevelt's second visit was more subdued.

"The lack of enthusiasm which Roosevelt met here was apparent from the very start. When he appeared on the platform of his car possibly a half dozen people started to clap but the others did not take it up and the applause soon died out. As soon as he stepped from the car he followed his usual custom and went to shake hands with his engineer and thank him for the safe trip," the *Gettysburg Times* reported.

George Kieffer and John Pitzer took Roosevelt and 1500 NBLE delegates on a battlefield tour. They walked from Oak Ridge to the cut near Reynold's Woods. Another train met them there and carried them out to Devil's Den.

They then walked to the luncheon tent where the ladies of St. James Lutheran Church served lunch. After the meal Roosevelt, Swope and Stone made some short remarks that were well received by the group, which was primarily made up of engineers. Roosevelt spoke about the railroads and their mission, though politics popped up.

"When Mr. Stone invited me last fall to come to Gettysburg for today," Roosevelt told the crowd, "I replied, 'By George, that's a place I will go.'"

"Put your hat in the ring, Teddy," someone yelled from the back of the tent, referring to Roosevelt running once again for President.

"It's there now and it will stay there," Roosevelt said as he raised his black slouch hat off his head.

Following the luncheon the crowd headed toward Soldiers' National Cemetery for the Memorial Day program. Roosevelt and the other guests took part in the Memorial Day parade before heading to the cemetery where he was one of the speakers.

"The veterans of the Civil War," Roosevelt said, "not only left us a united country, united forever, and not only left us the priceless heritage of the memories of valorous self-sacrifice shown in the Civil War, but also by their careers and their whole attitude in the war and after the war, have taught us lessons which we should apply to ourselves in civil life. During the war they showed that mixture of intense and lofty idealism with sound, practical common sense, which is as essential to a nation's success in peas as in war."

President Theodore Roosevelt poses for a picture at the train station during his 1912 visit. Photo courtesy of the Adams County Historical Society.

There had been concerns that the keynote speeches at Memorial Day had been becoming more and more political. However, Roosevelt knew where and when politics should be played and it wasn't at the National Cemetery. His political comments had been few, and he made them at the luncheon.

Roosevelt concluded his remarks at the cemetery by saying, "If we refuse to face the fact that there are great existing evils, and that we must try to solve them, then we shall prepare disaster to ourselves in the future: and we shall no less prepare disaster four ourselves if we fail to work with Lincoln's broad kindliness of spirit, toward all our fellow citizens with malice toward none, with charity to all striving resolutely to accomplish our ends but frowning on all vindictiveness and doing everything in our power to prevent rankling hatred."

Following the ceremony, Roosevelt was driven back to the train station to catch another train.

"Even at the station as the train pulled out there was little applause, comparatively little cheering and, barring the reception at the ten and the cemetery, Mr. Roosevelt's welcome by the Memorial Day crowds had a distinct chilly," the *Gettysburg Times* noted.

However, the newspaper also noted that the day overall had been very successful.

"Fifteen thousand people visited Gettysburg on Thursday May 30, making the day one of the most notable in point of numbers that the town has had for many years. It compared favorably with such days as those which witnessed the dedication of the new Pennsylvania monument, the Regular monument dedication with President Taft as the attraction, and Memorial Day, 1904, the time of Roosevelt's last visit when several details from the Regular Army and Marine Band—that didn't play—were the drawing cards," the newspaper reported.

Vandals Attack Monuments on Multiple Nights

I n 1913, Gettysburg prepared to welcome tens of thousands of veterans back to the battlefield to remember the 50th anniversary of the battle and to celebrate the peace between north and south. Amidst this hopeful time, someone let it be known he didn't agree.

"The worst outrage ever committed on the Gettysburg Battlefield was perpetrated early Tuesday evening in the vicinity of Round Top and the Valley of Death when three handsome monuments were battered and broken by a vandal who evidently used a heavy hammer for his work," the *Gettysburg Times* reported on March 5.

The granite 5th Corps Monument on Sedgwick Avenue stands six feet tall and has a Maltese Cross on four sides. The vandal knocked the top of the monument off and damaged the corners where the Maltese Crosses met.

The 10-foot-tall granite 37th Massachusetts Volunteer Infantry Monument features a tree with a rifle propped against it, a bag, and other pieces of equipment. The vandal broke the rifle off.

The granite 96th Pennsylvania Infantry Monument features a soldier laying on his stomach and holding his rifle at the ready. The vandal destroyed the soldier's face and the visor of his cap.

The damage was discovered early in the evening of the March 4. The pieces of the monuments that had been knocked off had been left on the ground around the monuments. They were cataloged, collected, and taken to storage.

Col. Emmor Cope, who was in charge of the park, said, "This is the worst thing that has ever happened to battlefield property, and we sincerely hope that all good citizens will put forth every effort to assist the commission in learning the names of the persons concerned."

The soldier on top of the monument dedicated to the 96th Pennsylvania Volunteers was one of many Gettysburg monuments damaged in 1913.

No motive could be determined for the destruction, although rumors abounded. "The kindest interpretation which has been put upon it is that some one mentally deranged must have visited the section and that the crime was the result of a disordered mind," the *Gettysburg Times* reported.

The next morning residents woke to discover that six more monuments of the battlefield's 500 monuments had been vandalized; "two of them being among the best pieces of sculpture on the battlefield," according to the *Gettysburg Times*.

The granite 40th New York Infantry Monument features a soldier with a rifle concealed behind rocks. The vandal battered the soldier's face, crushed his foot, and broke his rifle.

The granite 1st Vermont Brigade monument depicts a lion with his mouth open laying atop a pedestal. The vandal broke the lion's lower jaw off and crushed his tail.

The monuments for the 6th Maine Volunteers, the Wisconsin Volunteer Infantry, 6th New Jersey Volunteer Infantry, and 49th Pennsylvania Infantry all had their corners and rifle hammers chipped away.

The pieces were collected and taken to the National Park Commission office. The goal was to repair the monuments, but each one had to be evaluated to see if it was possible.

One possible reason for the vandalism – a man on a drunken rampage – was dismissed because it was doubtful such a person would have done the same thing two nights in a row. More and more people believed someone was doing the damage out of spite for being fired from or not hired for a battlefield job. However, no person seemed to fit that description.

"Numerous false rumors gain currency about town almost every hour in connection with the vandalism," the *Gettysburg Times* reported. "One of these reports more monuments desecrated almost hourly while another is that the guilty party has been apprehended."

One reason no one suggested but seems obvious is that someone who supported the South caused the damage. All of the damaged monuments honored Union forces.

The park usually had five men who worked on the battlefield overnight. Eight more men were added to the overnight detail to prevent additional vandalism. A $100 reward (about $2,600 today) was offered for the capture of the vandal. Since the destruction was a federal crime, the vandal also faced a $10 to $1,000 fine for each monument and/or 15 days to 1 year in prison.

Meanwhile, all clues were investigated to try and find the culprit. Measurements taken of the damage led investigators to believe the vandal had used the butt end of an ax. Footprints and hoof prints were also found in near the damage of some of the monuments.

News of the vandalism spread to other areas of the country, and editorial pages criticized the vandals. The *Harrisburg Telegraph* compared the damage to slashing classic paintings. "The sight of these mutilated memorials will wound the old soldiers deeply, and there is not sufficient time to repair the damage, even though there were unlimited money at hand to do it," the newspaper reported.

It was determined that all of the damaged monuments could be repaired using a mixture made up of wax, dust from the original granite used in the monuments, and other materials that were boiled together. The result was supposed to be harder than the original and last 50-60 years.

"When cooled it has the exact appearance of the original and can be carved to the design of the monument before damaged," the *Gettysburg Times* reported.

The cost of the repairs was estimated to be $7,032 (about $180,000 today). Portions of seven of the monuments were sent away to be repaired by Van Amringe Granite Company in Boston. "Where possible, the damaged portions will be sent back to the quarries from which they were originally cut, and the stone and work will be duplicated as nearly as possible," the *Gettysburg Times* reported.

The pieces were then returned to Gettysburg to be attached to the original. The repairs to the 5th Corps and 6th Maine monuments were done entirely onsite by L. H. Meals.

As the days crept on without a suspect, many editorial writers placed the blame on Gettysburg and its residents.

Despite the outrage, no one was ever charged with the destruction.

First Confederate State Monument Dedicated at Gettysburg

E ven as a new war threatened to break out, peace was still being made over the Civil War in 1917.

In 1911, the Commonwealth of Virginia appropriated $50,000 for a monument on the Gettysburg battlefield. It would be the first monument erected by a southern state at Gettysburg and the hope had been that it would dedicated during the events of the 50th anniversary of the battle in 1913.

Frederick W. Sievers won the contract to build the monument with a design that won out over 40 other competitors. The monument design featured seven figures that represented three branches of the army during the Battle of Gettysburg – artillery, cavalry and infantry. They were on a pedestal on which was surmounted a statue of Confederate Gen. Robert E. Lee astride his horse, Traveler.

Sievers studied at the Royal Academy of Fine Arts in Rome, Italy, and the Académie Julian in Paris, France.

He created the figure of Lee from photographs and life masks of the general. So dedicated was he to making sure that both Lee and Traveler looked like they had in life Sievers travelled to Lexington, Va., to study Traveler's skeleton, which was preserved at Washington and Lee University. Sievers found a horse the same size as Traveler and took measurements of the horse so that the sculpture would appear authentic.

"One of the details Sievers included on Traveler is that the ears appear 'perked' forward as if listening to the sound of a distant battle," according to the website, *StoneSentinels.com.*

Frederick W. Sievers sculpted the first Confederate monument dedicated on the Gettysburg battlefield in 1917. Author photo.

Below Lee, around the base are the seven soldiers representing the men of the South.

"I have selected the characters from men of different degrees of social standing because I wanted to recall the fact that patriotism places rich and poor, the aristocrat and the son of the soil, on equal footing," Sievers said. "The most interesting feature, from my point of view, is the departure from the stereotyped manner in representing the arms of service with the usual figures in meaningless poses on different sides of the pedestal, and I believe that my treatment of the subject is original."

Frederick W. Sievers

The website *GettysburgBattlefieldTours.com* describes the soldiers this way: "First, there are two riflemen, one symbolic of a professional man, the other a mechanic. Beside them, a man who was an artist now aims a pistol. In the center, a boy on horseback raises the Confederate flag. To his right, a businessman swings a bayonet, a farmer raises a rifle, and a youth sounds a bugle call. These smaller portraits remind us that they were more than just soldiers."

JAMES RADA, JR.

The Virginia Memorial along West Confederate Avenue is the largest Confederate monument at Gettysburg. It stands 41 feet tall. The General Lee and Traveler sculpture is 14 feet tall.

When it became clear that the monument wouldn't be ready in time for the Grand Reunion, the granite pedestal without the sculptures was dedicated on June 30, 1913. The completed monument was dedicated on June 8, 1917.

The State of Virginia appropriated funds to send veterans and other guests to the event. The original plan had also included sending a couple regiments of soldiers, but their priority became preparing to fight in what would become World War I. In their place, 350 cadets from the Virginia Military Institute attended. It was estimated that about 3,500 people attended.

"Interest throughout the South is widespread in the Gettysburg event and nothing short of a catastrophe can prevent the dedication bringing a great crowd," the *Gettysburg Times* reported.

As the trains bearing the Confederate veterans and special guests arrived, bands playing music met them. A town escort led them through Gettysburg to the monument.

Virginia Carter, a niece of Gen. Robert E Lee, was among the special guests. She pulled the cords that allowed the flags covering the sculpture to fall away as the band played. The immediate response was long and thunderous applause. Then the *Gettysburg Times* noted an interesting thing that happened.

"For minutes after the flags had been removed hundreds of the men stood in mute admiration of the sculptor's work, and in deep reverence as memory took them back to the days of more than half a century ago when they were led through the trying days, months, and years of the Civil War."

Virginia Governor Henry C. Stuart presented the completed memorial to the Assistant Secretary of War.

Gettysburg's
Least-Visited Monument

A long the winding Howard Avenue in Gettysburg, you pass monuments that mark the actions of military units such as the 107th Ohio Infantry and the 58th New York Infantry. The monuments sit so close to the road you don't even have to leave the comfort of an air-conditioned car to read the inscriptions on the stone blocks. At the crest of the road, a cluster of monuments, statues, cannon, and a flagpole mark the events that took place in July 1863 on Barlow Knoll.

From that crest, you can look northeast down the slope of Barlow Knoll to the tree line along Rock Creek. Within those trees is arguably the least-visited monument on the Gettysburg Battlefield. Although the National Park Service keeps no visitor statistics for monuments, this monument is so isolated that you have to know what you are looking for to find it.

There is no road to pull up alongside a tall, sculpted statue. There is no trail graded and well-marked that you can stroll along. You won't even find a sign to give you directions to marker.

"You could definitely make a case that it's the least visited marker," said Katie Lawhon with the National Park Service.

Little fighting took place at the marker's location, but you can't even tell that from the inscription on the small granite block to the 54th New York Infantry. It reads: "A detail of 45 men from this regiment occupied this position July 1st 1863."

The 54th New York Infantry

The 54th New York Infantry recruited primarily Germans from Brooklyn and New York City who mustered into the service near Hudson City, N. J., between September 5 and October 16, 1861. The unit also received one company of the McClellan Infantry.

From New Jersey, the unit served near Washington, D.C. until April 1862. It was then sent into Virginia under the command of General Fremont. The 54th fought in the Battle of Cross Keys and in the Chancellorville Campaign, according to *The Union army: a history of military affairs in the loyal states, 1861-65 -- records of the regiments in the Union army -- cyclopedia of battles -- memoirs of commanders and soldiers.*

At Gettysburg, Maj. Stephen Kovacs commanded the 54th New York at Gettysburg, although he was captured on July 1. The unit was attached to the 1st Brigade, 1st Division, 11th Corps of the Army of the Potomac.

The granite stone below Barlow Knoll is an advance marker that shows where a detachment of soldiers was placed on the south side of Rock Creek to delay the enemy if they could. The New Yorkers engaged John Brown Gordon's Brigade from Georgia, according to the Gettysburg Daily website.

"Accounts of the 54th's action here are scarce," according to Gettysburg Daily. "The 68th New York and 153rd Pennsylvania also had skirmishers in this area. At first the Union troops fought well. An account from the 61st Georgia states that the skirmish line of the New Yorkers and Pennsylvanians was difficult to move."

The Georgians did eventually push the Union men back,

though, and the 54th detachment retreated to join up with its larger command.

Hidden in overgrown woods, the marker to the 54th New York Infantry has been called the least-visited monument on the Gettysburg Battlefield. Author photo.

Contrast this small marker to the much larger monument to the 54th New York that is southeast of Gettysburg on Wainwright Avenue (and seen from the road). "This monument to Hiram Barney Rifles" depicts Heinrich Michel in bas refief. He was killed carrying the company colors on July 2, 1863, the day following the detachment's actions near Barlow Knoll. During the fighting here, Lt. Ernst Both was in command, since Major Kovacs was a Confederate prisoner.

Of the 216 soldiers of the 54th New York Infantry who took the field at Gettysburg, 7 were killed, 47 wounded, and 48 went missing.

Following the Battle of Gettysburg, the 54th New York Infantry camped near Hagerstown, Md., until August when it was sent to Charleston Harbor in South Carolina. It was stationed on Folly Island and took part in the siege of Fort Wagner and the bombardment of Fort Sumter. During the summer of 1864, the unit fought on James Island where 20 men died. It remained in the Charleston area until it was mustered out on April 14, 1866.

Getting There

Getting to the monument itself is a battle. From the top of Barlow Knoll, you walk downhill to the trees about 100 yards away. This is no easy feat if you have to tramp through the grass when it is waist high.

At the tree line, you have to find a game trail that leads back into the woods. If you don't know what you're looking for, you can get lost.

The trail is overgrown and winds back and forth over fallen timber, across dry waterways, and occasionally passing the carcass of a dead deer.

"Years ago, it had a path to it, but it was moved," Lawhon said.

Grass surrounding the monument nearly hides it, but there it sits, visited less than a handful of times each year because you have to know where you're going to find this monument. Even knowing where it's located, you could pass within feet, never realizing that one of Gettysburg's 1328 monuments sits in such an isolated inaccessible location.

Returning to your car from the marker is even a greater chore. You must wade through about 100 yards of grass and brush just to get out of the trees. Then you have to climb Barlow Knoll. This can be quite a challenge if the tall grass is bent toward you like pikemen with their pikes lowered to meet an enemy charge. Because the grass was waist high to start, it now reaches your stomach and chest because of the incline. Lawhon pointed out that whether the slope is mowed depends on the time of year and what crops might be grown nearby.

Other Less-Visited Monuments

The 54th New York Infantry advance marker isn't the only out-of-the-way marker. Not all of the fighting during the Civil War battle took place in locations where it is feasible to have a road. Here are other monuments on the battlefield that don't see many visitors because of their isolated locations.

- Hupp's Battery Salem Virginia Artillery Marker in the woods north of the railroad cut on Oak Ridge.
- Col. George Willard's marker east of Plum Run that marks where he was killed.
- 16th Pennsylvania monument on Clapsaddle Road.
- The Pennsylvania cavalry monument on Low Dutch Road.

50TH & 75TH ANNIVERSARIES

Three Stories from the 50ᵗʰ

T he 1913 anniversary of the Battle of Gettysburg marked 50 years since the battle. Most of the living veterans of the Civil War were in their seventies. For many of them, the 50th anniversary would be their last chance to attend a major anniversary of the battle.

An estimated 56,000 veterans came to Gettysburg to remember the War Between the States and put their former animosities asides. The reunion marked memorial dedications, the cyclorama opening in Gettysburg, and a few other stories that aren't easily found in history books.

SPAM

Though SPAM canned ham wasn't officially introduced until 1937, a form of the canned, boneless meat was first introduced during the 50th reunion at Gettysburg.

"In order to handle the group, which far exceeded the original attendance estimates, an entirely new system of supply had to be improvised. During the encampment, selected cuts of fresh beef were chilled and boned in packing houses, and then packed in lined wooden shipping boxes," according to the U.S. Army Quartermaster Museum.

The cases of canned meat were refrigerated and shipped on trains to Gettysburg where the camp cooks used them to feed the veterans. The cooks would slice the meat into steaks they would fry and broil for entrees.

"The importance of the Gettysburg experience went more or less unrecognized until shipping shortages in World War I forced Army subsistence personnel to look for new ways to try to conserve space onboard cargo ships going to Europe," according to the U.S. Army Quartermaster Museum.

At that time, Lt. Jay C. Hormel of the U.S. Army Quartermaster Corps returned from France to develop a large-scale production system. With the success of the system, canned meat became a staple of army field rations beginning in World War I. Hormel's production and supply system became SPAM and Hormel became president of the George A. Hormel and Hormel Company in Austin, Minn.

Jay C. Hormel conceived of SPAM when he served as a quartermaster during the 1913 Gettysburg anniversary. Photo courtesy of Wikimedia Commons.

The aging survivors of Pickett's Charge re-enact their famous charge. Photo courtesy of the U.S. Militaria Forums.

The First Gettysburg Movie

The first movie about Gettysburg, *The Battle of Gettysburg,* made its debut at Walter's Theatre on June 26, 1913, just as the first veterans were arriving for the Grand Reunion. It was a black-and-white silent film. All prints of the movie have been lost to time, but according to *IMDB.com,* the 50-minute movie tells the story of a young woman's sweetheart who fights for the Union Army while her brother fights for the Confederate Army. They come face-to-face during the Battle of Gettysburg.

The movie stars Willard Mack and Charles K. French. Mack played Abraham Lincoln in the film. Charles Giblyn and Thomas H. Hince directed.

Though considered a "lost" film, some of the battle footage can be seen in the comedy, *Cohen Saves the Flag.* The battle sequences were shot together in Malibu, California. Also, according to the website, *The Silent Era,* a version of the film was screened in France in 1973.

Fireworks

Although there would be activities on July 4, the evening of July 3, 1913, marked the 50th anniversary of the last day of the Battle of Gettysburg. It was marked with a large fireworks display shot off from the top of Little Roundtop that cost an estimated $10,000.

Because of the thousands of returning veterans to Gettysburg, the military built a temporary encampment on the battlefield. Photo courtesy of the Library of Congress.

One newspaper article reported, "The display began with a wonderfully well arranged electric display which lighted the sky like the bursting of bombs as the cannon roared. This continued for fully 10 minutes, with the burning of red and blue light in such quantities that the sky for miles and miles around was lighted. then the electrical display was temporarily stopped and only read and blue lights were burned."

Among the features was a 200-foot-wide by 120-foot-tall American flag and a figure of a Union and Confederate soldier shaking hands. It included 100 pyrotechnists who shot off 4,000 shells ranging in diameter from 3 to 30 inches.

"Perhaps the most interesting feature of the entire display—the one that will bring the thrill of the days of '61 to the veterans who have been spared for this great reunion—will be the exact reproduction of the signal code of the Union Army—sixteen set pieces in red, white and blue fire. Radiant in gorgeous fire will also burn the corps badges of the Army of the Potomac and that of the Confederate forces identified with the Gettysburg battle," the *Gettysburg Times* reported.

A special balloon shell released the flag display so that the flag floated over the veterans.

An estimated 14,000 cars packed into the area filled with spectators who wanted to see the fireworks. The Pennsylvania Reunion Commission report noted that they double parked along both sides of every from in the area and when the drivers turned on their headlights, it "seemed as though thousands of gigantic fireflies were silently, swiftly moving through the darkness of night, throughout the great battlefield's length and breadth..." according to the report of the Pennsylvania Commission, which put together the reunion.

The U.S. Cavalry and Pennsylvania State Police directed the traffic that did not clear out until well after midnight.

The sound of the show was so loud that it frightened many of the veterans. A few of the veterans were thrown back to 1863 and shouted, "Down, boys! Lie down! Steady."

Batavia resident Alvin J. Fox fought in Lockwood's Brigade during the Battle of Gettysburg. "The sounds of the firing of aerial bombs and the explosion of fireworks last Thursday night reminded him, he said, of the sounds of battle," *The Daily News* reported.

Civil War veterans finally put their differences behind them at the 50th anniversary of the Battle of Gettysburg. Photo courtesy of the Pennsylvania Reunion Commission Report.

Gettysburg Gets a Cyclorama

I MAX and 3-D movies both have the cyclorama to thank
for their existence. Cycloramas were an early method of
trying to achieve what both IMAX and 3-D movies do,
which is to bring the viewer into the picture.

In Adams County, many people think of the Gettysburg
Cyclorama as unique or as the only cyclorama. It's neither.

Cycloramas were an art form practiced primarily in the
late 19th century.

"These massive oil-on-canvas paintings were displayed in
special auditoriums and enhanced with landscaped fore-
grounds sometimes featuring trees, grasses, fences and even
life-sized figures. The result was a three-dimensional effect
that surrounded the viewers who stood on a central platform,
literally placing them in the center of the great historic scene," according to the Gettysburg NMP website.

The Gettysburg Cyclorama, for instance, is 359 feet
around and 27 feet tall with dirt, grass, and some props leading from the center of the room where it is displayed and
blending with the edge of the painting. Given the size of such
paintings, they were used to depict events that had a lot to
see, such as battles or stories.

At one point, Europe and America displayed hundreds of
cycloramas. Sadly, most of them have been destroyed over
the years.

French artist Paul Philippoteaux works on "The Battle of Gettysburg" cyclorama painting. Photo courtesy of Wikimedia Commons.

"The 'Battle of Gettysburg' Cyclorama at Gettysburg National Military Park is one that has survived. This fantastic painting brings the fury of the final Confederate assault on July 3, 1863, to life, providing the viewer with a sense of what occurred at the battle long touted as the turning point of the Civil War," according to the National Park Service website.

One of the many scenes depicted in the cyclorama painting of the Battle of Gettysburg. Courtesy of Wikimedia Commons.

French artist Paul Philippoteaux painted "The Battle of Gettysburg", which highlights Pickett's Charge. Philippoteaux visited Gettysburg in April 1882 and spent several weeks studying the battlefield, making preliminary sketches, researching the battle and taking photographs. He even interviewed survivors of the battle to hear their stories. Then with five assistants, he spent a year and a half painting the battle. The finished work was nearly 100 yards long and weighed six tons.

Four versions of the painting were done. The first was originally shown in Chicago on October 22, 1883.

"It was at Chicago for nine years and while there cleared almost a million [visitors]," *The Gettysburg Times* reported when it was announced that Gettysburg would get a painting.

In the minutes of the Seventeenth Annual Meeting and Re-Union of the United Confederate Veterans, Adj. Gen. William Mickle, noted that he saw two Confederate veterans brought to tears at the sight of the painting.

A 2013 article in *The Atlantic* was critical of the painting because it did not show the context of the war, but author Yoni Appelbaum also wrote that the painting was so detailed and so powerful that, "Its version of the conflict proved so alluring, in fact, that it changed the way America remembered the Civil War."

The Chicago version is not the one on display in Gettysburg. That painting was lost for decades until it was rediscovered in 1965 and purchased by a group of North Carolina investors.

The second painting was first shown in Boston. When it was replaced temporarily with another cyclorama painting in 1891, it was shown for a time in Philadelphia. However, when "The Battle of Gettysburg" returned to Boston, it wasn't immediately put on display and was damaged while in storage.

Albert Hahne of Newark, N. J., purchased this damaged version in 1910. He displayed it in Newark; Baltimore, Md.; New York City, N.Y. and Washington D.C.

On September 3, 1912, ground was broken for a cyclorama building on Baltimore Street in Gettysburg near the entrance to Soldiers' National Cemetery. It was during the 50th battle reunion that the Gettysburg Cyclorama opened for the public.

The National Park Service purchased it in 1942 and moved it to a new location in Ziegler's Grove when the old visitor's center opened in 1961.

It remained there until 2005 when it was closed, underwent extensive renovation and moved to a new location within the new National Park Visitors' Center on Baltimore Street. Olin Conservation, the company restoring the painting, found original pieces of it that had been thought lost. These pieces were restored and added an additional 12 feet of the painting and restored 14 vertical feet of sky. The new cyclorama opened in September 2008.

A third version of the painting that was originally shown in Philadelphia was destroyed and the fourth version, which was originally shown in Brooklyn, N.Y., is currently lost.

"No other American cyclorama ever came close to matching the popularity of Philippoteaux's *Gettysburg*. It had an educational purpose and also offered a voyeuristic thrill," Appelbaum wrote.

This was the home of the Gettysburg Cyclorama for many years until it moved to the Gettysburg National Military Park Visitors Center. Photo courtesy of Library of Congress.

Gettysburg was the State Capital for Five Days

H istory books tell you that the Commonwealth of Pennsylvania has had three state capitals over the years. In Colonial times, the statehouse was in Philadelphia. It moved to Lancaster for 13 years from 1799 to 1812 before moving to its present location in Harrisburg, and it has been there ever since.

Except for a five-day period in 1938.

"Historic Gettysburg will become the seat of Pennsylvania's state government for the first time in the history of the Commonwealth during the 75th battle anniversary observance, June 29 to July 6," the *Gettysburg Times* reported.

Because of the expected crowds, the borough had worked to make a good impression on visitors and veterans alike. Workmen had repaired all of the streets leading into Gettysburg and removed any weeds. Flags were draped across the streets — Chambersburg, York, Baltimore, and Carlisle — leading from the town square. Business owners filled their store windows with displays about the anniversary. Public buildings were festooned with flags. The borough had even arranged for many of the buildings to receive a fresh coat of paint.

The *Gettysburg Times* reported, "Gettysburg will present its brightest and gayest appearance in 25 years."

The Civil War veterans' camp was constructed on the north end of Gettysburg College and also on some adjacent privately owned property. The Pennsylvania Blue and Gray Planning Commission housed the veterans in tents just as had been done during the 1913 reunion when more than 6,500 tents were erected in a temporary camp south of Gettysburg. Although far fewer veterans attended the 75th anniversary reunion, there wasn't enough room for all of them in hotels and constructing wooden barracks would have been too costly.

Aerial view of the veteran's camp for the 1938 Gettysburg reunion. Photo courtesy of Wikimedia Commons.

Planning for the event had begun in 1935, but actual construction of the camp hadn't started until April 26, 1938. Boardwalk streets were laid out in a grid fashion. Union veteran tents were on lettered streets. Confederate veteran tents lined numbered streets. Mummasburg Road split the Confederate and Union sections of the camp.

During the first five days of July while there was lots of activity going on in Gettysburg honoring the veterans who had returned for the last great reunion of veterans, including army encampments and a visit from President Franklin D. Roosevelt to dedicate the Peace Light Memorial. With all of this activity in Gettysburg, Governor George Howard Earle, III, moved his staff to temporary headquarters in Gettysburg.

Gov. George Howard Earle addresses a gathering during the 1938 Gettysburg anniversary. From unknown publication.

The temporary capital was set up in Huber Hall on the campus of Gettysburg College. The college property bordered the area where the veterans' camp had been erected.

The college buildings also served as the headquarters for the Pennsylvania Reunion Commission and an official reception center. Other college buildings were also used for the

75th anniversary reunion of the Battle of Gettysburg. Glatfelter Hall became a general headquarters, Pennsylvania Hall became a hospital and nurses' quarters, McKnight and Weidensall Hall housed the media, the Eddie Plank Gymnasium housed the Army band, and the Pennsylvania State Motor Patrolmen stayed on the football practice field.

Final inspection of the Pennsylvania State Motor Police during the 1938 Gettysburg anniversary. From unknown publication.

"Health, Highways, Forest and Waters, and Public Instruction sent small contingents to aid in supervision and presentation of the vast observance program," the *Gettysburg Times* noted.

Also, 450 state motor patrolmen and 500 National Guardsmen set up their temporary headquarters in Gettysburg. From this location, Pennsylvania government conducted its business for nearly a week amid the hoopla and spectacle that was the 75th anniversary of the Battle of Gettysburg.

It is interesting to note that the actual Battle of Gettysburg in 1863 with the approach of General Lee's army only caused a preparation for moving the state capital elsewhere, whereas, a reunion 75 years later did cause the capital to be moved.

A 95-Year-Old Remembers the 75ᵗʰ Anniversary

T he last day of June 1938 14-year-old Chuck Caldwell and his father drove from their home in Orrville, Ohio, to Gettysburg.

It was a legendary, almost mythical, place to the young teenager. Gettysburg was a town that was forever stuck in its past because of its connection with the pivotal battle of the Civil War. Chuck knew the names of the generals and officers who had fought here as well as he knew the names of his favorite baseball players. Lee. Meade. Chamberlain and so many others. Some were considered heroes, others villains, but they were all legends in Chuck's mind.

Seventy-five years after the famous battle, the population was around 5,800, and that's only if you counted permanent residents. In the summers, the population was at least double that as tourists visited the battlefield driving across the field where armies had once fought, and thousands of soldiers died. Now hundreds of monuments had sprung up across the land like lonely sentinels to remind those visitors they were on hallowed ground.

In the 1930s, those whom the Civil War had not taken were slowly being picked off by time. Isaac Caldwell had died in 1885. By 1938, only about 8,000 Civil War veterans were still alive out of the more than 3.2 million men who had served in the armed forces. Chuck wished that he could have met them all. He gave it his best effort, but there was only so much that a fourteen-year-old could do.

His father, George, who was the pastor at the Orrville Presbyterian Church, often spoke at other churches or at meetings of pastors held outside of Orrville. Whenever he did, George would pour through the local newspapers and ask about whether any Civil War veterans were living in the towns he visited. If there were, George would call them and make an appointment to stop by and get a picture, autograph, and some biographical information about them. Then he would give Chuck the mementos when he returned home.

Family members who knew of Chuck's interest would save stories about Civil War veterans that popped up in their hometown newspapers from time to time. They would clip them and mail them off to Chuck. He would open the envelopes like they were Christmas presents and read the stories looking for new information and names. Then he would paste the clippings into a scrapbook.

Chuck would often write to the veterans whose addresses he could find. He would pepper them with questions about their service in the Civil War, the battles they had fought, the hardships they had endured, and the training they had received. A good number of the veterans wrote him back. Chuck corresponded with some of them right until they died.

With the 75th anniversary of the Civil War beginning in 1936, many newspapers ran features about the veterans who lived in their circulation areas. The articles allowed the veterans to recount their wartime experiences. Chuck had read as many of the articles as he could find so he had been overjoyed to discover that he and his father would travel to Gettysburg for the last, significant anniversary.

Chuck Caldwell and Confederate Civil War veteran Stephen Howe in 1938. Photo courtesy of Chuck Caldwell.

Most of the veterans had come earlier the same day that Chuck and his father had arrived, but they came to Gettysburg on twelve special Pullman trains. Some of the men were so frail they had to be carried off the trains on stretchers.

The Gettysburg that the Caldwells drove into in 1938 was a small town crammed with people. Cars crept along the roads, bumper to bumper. Tents pitched in open fields formed small communities. People clustered on sidewalks, reminding Chuck of pictures he had seen of major cities like New York and Philadelphia. Many of the people on the sidewalks were probably from those cities and thinking about how uncrowded Gettysburg was.

Because of the expected crowds, the borough had worked to make a good impression on visitors and veterans alike. In the weeks leading up to the reunion, workmen had repaired all of the streets leading into Gettysburg and removed any weeds along the sidewalks. Flags draped across the streets—Chambersburg, York, Baltimore, and Carlisle—leading from the town square. Businesses filled their windows with displays about the anniversary. Public buildings were festooned with flags. The borough had even arranged for many of the buildings to receive a fresh coat of paint. At night, the town was lit up with red, white, and blue lights.

The *Gettysburg Times* reported, "Gettysburg will present its brightest and gayest appearance in 25 years." One Confederate veteran's wife said all of the activity and decorations in town reminded her of a huge street carnival.

Tim Murphy of Harrisburg was a big reason for this declaration. Murphy had worked in event promotion and decorating for over twenty-five years. He had learned showmanship from working with the Barnum and Bailey's Circus and Buffalo Bill's Wild West Show. He had also decorated Washington, D.C. for the inaugurations of Franklin D. Roosevelt, Calvin Coolidge, and Warren G. Harding. Perhaps most importantly, he had helped decorate Gettysburg for the Grand Reunion of 1913 when 57,000 Civil War veterans had come to Gettysburg to remember the battle and their days in the Blue or the Gray.

Chuck's head swung back and forth looking for Civil War veterans in the crowd, but he saw no one whom he could point to and say, "I want to meet him!" Most of the men wore nice suits, though some of them had forsaken their jackets because of the heat. They were far too young to have served in the Civil War. Chuck saw men in brown uniforms, but they were modern soldiers.

While the Caldwells hadn't needed to make a room reservation two years ago, this year, each innkeeper, tourist court owner, and motel manager with whom they inquired told them the same thing. They had arrived too late in the day. All of their rooms were filled. Try back around lunch time tomorrow.

With each rejection, it looked like it was less likely that Chuck and his father would find a place to stay for the night at least in Gettysburg. Both of them dreaded getting back in the car to drive on to Biglerville, New Oxford, or Emmitsburg in search of a room.

A farmer saved the day. George Caldwell talked to the man on the street, hoping to get a lead where he could find a room in town. The farmer agreed with everyone else that all of the rooms tourists visiting for the 75th anniversary of the battle filled up all of the rooms in town. Then he offered the Caldwells the use of his old chicken coop, which was vacant.

That was why Chuck woke up in a chicken coop on July 1, 1938, rather than a bed. He shook his father awake, and they washed up in the farmer's house, changed clothes and drove back into Gettysburg.

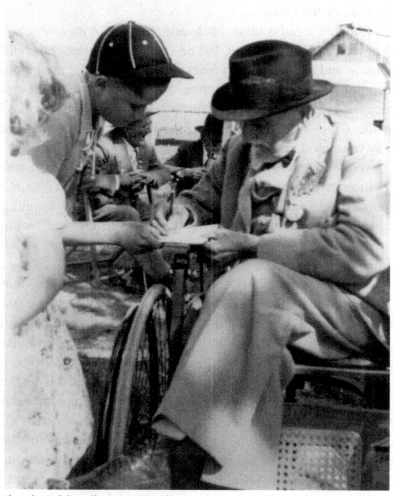

Chuck Caldwell gets a Civil War veteran to sign his autograph book during the 1938 Gettysburg anniversary. Photo courtesy of Chuck Caldwell.

One night in a chicken coop had been enough for the Caldwells. George made sure he took part of the afternoon to revisit the tourist camps and hotels in town until they found a place to stay that offered them a real bed with no ventilation through the floor.

The Civil War veterans weren't staying in hotels or inns, either. Even though their rooms were tents, they were five-star accommodations compared to a chicken coop.

The veterans' camp had been constructed on the north end of Gettysburg College and also on some adjacent privately owned property. The Pennsylvania Blue and Gray Planning Commission had housed the veterans in tents just as had been done during the 1913 reunion when over 6,500 tents had been erected in a temporary camp south of Gettysburg. Although far fewer veterans attended the 75th-anniversary reunion, there wasn't enough room for all of them in hotels and constructing wooden barracks would have been too costly.

Planning for the 75th-anniversary reunion had begun in 1935, but men of the Civilian Conservation Corps hadn't started construction of the camp until April 26, 1938.

Boardwalk streets were laid out in a grid fashion. Union veteran tents were on lettered streets from Biglerville Road to Mummasburg Road. Confederate veteran tents lined num-bered streets from Mummasburg Road to the Reading Rail-road. Mummasburg Road split the Confederate and Union sections of the camp.

Each veteran was given either a United States flag or a Confederate flag to display in front of his tent if he wanted to do so. Annette Tucker, wife of a Confederate veteran at the reunion, wrote, "At the time I felt so loyal to the Government for making this meeting possible and for all the favors they were bestowing upon us that it didn't seem proper to display the Confederate flag, not even at the Reunion, even if we were permitted this privilege, so I folded mine to bring home for a souvenir and perhaps use at our own U. D. C. meetings."

Short wooden walks ran off the streets at right angles leading to the nine-foot by nine-foot tents. Each tent had two cots; one for the veteran and one for his attendant. The tents had wash stands and electric lights in them. They also had rain flys in front of them that offered shade so that the veteran could sit outside and talk to his neighbors or greet passersby like Chuck.

"It was a thrill to be able to see both armies together at one time. It was just too much. I would have walked from home to be there," Chuck said.

The men Chuck saw seemed frail compared to the soldiers they had been in their youth. Now in their nineties and even their hundreds, their hair, if they still had any, was white along with their sideburns, mustaches, and goatees. Many of them could stand for only short stretches and spent most of their time sitting in wheelchairs supplied by the reunion commission.

Most of them dressed in coats, vests, and neckties. Here and there, one veteran would dress in a shabby military uniform that was seventy-five years old. This was their special reunion and their time in the national spotlight. They wanted to make a good first impression with people they met.

For some, Gettysburg held such a special place in their hearts and minds they wanted to die on the battlefield. William W. Banks, a veteran who had served with Company H, Eighteenth Alabama Infantry, sent the Quartermaster General of the United States a telegram saying he represented a group of veterans "do desire to remain here on this hallowed hill till Gabriel shall call us to that eternal party where there is no strife, bitter hate, nor bloodshed and we are one for all and all for one."

Chuck Caldwell's view of the Peace Light dedication at
Gettysburg in 1938. Photo courtesy of Chuck Caldwell.

Because of his father's efforts to help Chuck meet living
Civil War veterans, Chuck had met some of these men be-

fore, if they lived close to Orrville. While those meetings stuck out in his young memory, the veterans rarely remembered meeting one particular young boy for a few minutes.

"They were close to 100 years old," Chuck said. "They wouldn't remember a little kid."

That didn't stop Chuck from approaching each veteran whom he could find. He carried his Brownie camera and an autograph book and looked more like a cub reporter than a tourist.

He would introduce himself and ask the veteran to sign his name and write the outfit he had served in during the war and his hometown. Chuck also asked his father to take a picture of the veteran and Chuck. The brown-haired and brown-eyed Chuck looks young in the pictures standing around five feet tall and as thin as a rail. He would ask the veteran any questions he could think of whether it was about a particular battle, military life, or their life after the war.

One man whom Chuck met was John C. Smith of Meridian, Mississippi. The 108-year-old veteran had fought with the 46th Georgia as the Confederates charged Little Roundtop at Gettysburg.

"Somewhere in that furious charge across the valley, a spent bullet thudded into Smith's cheek, and he spit it out into his powder-blackened hand and went on to fight across the hilltop and, finally, to give up to the Union reinforcements," *The Daily Herald* (Circleville, Ohio) reported.

The veterans' stories enraptured Chuck, and he could have listened to them for days on end. However, rain somewhat hampered his camp tour in the late afternoon and evening of Friday, July 1. Though the rainfall kept the temperature down, it also sent many people indoors. When the rain started, the camp headquarters sent a truckload of umbrellas to the veterans' camp. Over 2,000 umbrellas were distributed to veterans so they could continue touring the town in buses provided by the camp headquarters.

One of the first veterans whom Chuck met during the reunion was ninety-one-year-old Henry Rogers of Santa Monica, California. Rogers showed off his patriotism during one of the bus tours on the battlefield when he stood up and recited Lincoln's Gettysburg Address to the cheers of the other riders on the bus who were nearly all Civil War veterans themselves.

Rogers had served as a dispatch orderly with the Fortieth Illinois Infantry during the war. Three of his brothers had also served in the same company. During the Battle of Kenesaw Mountain in Georgia on June 27, 1864, Rogers and his brothers had charged against a regiment in which their uncle was a soldier.

Rogers' wife, Elizabeth, had accompanied her husband to the reunion and served as his attendant. She was seventy-eight years old, but still in good enough health to take care of her husband and serving as his attendant allowed them to share the same tent in the veterans' camp. Chuck struck up an acquaintance with Rogers and corresponded with the aged veteran until he died on November 20, 1938.

The main feature of July 1 was the opening ceremony at the Gettysburg College Stadium at 2 p.m. featuring U.S. Secretary of War Harry H. Woodring as the main speaker. One of the other speakers during the ceremony was the Reverend John M. Claypool of St. Louis, another veterans whom Chuck met and had sign his autograph book. Claypool was the commander of the United Confederate Veterans and a descendant of John Hancock.

Claypool's remarks were broadcast over national radio. He good-naturedly noted that if the South hadn't surrendered in 1865, it would have continued fighting using guerilla warfare still today, but Southerners had been too high-minded to pursue fighting a lost cause.

"We can't hold anything against each other," Claypool said. "I speak as the representative of real Americans and as a real American myself. God bless you all."

That second night in Gettysburg, Chuck, and his father slept in a bed in a room in a tourist camp, but Chuck was awake early in the morning ready to go visiting the veterans' camp. Many of the tents were empty as their occupants were out touring the battlefield. Among the occupied tents, Chuck often found the aged veterans sleeping.

He and his father toured the Union camp first and then crossed the street to the Confederate camp.

"I could hardly wait to get to the Confederate camp because there were so many fewer of them," Chuck recalled.

During one of his trips to the Confederate camp, young Chuck met O. Richard Gillette, who had served in Davis's Brigade with the 2nd Mississippi. Though he fought in some major battles during the war, the only time he was wounded was at the Battle of Antietam.

"A piece of shrapnel hit me in the knee. It didn't hurt me much, but the worst of it was it ruined my britches," Gillette told the *Gettysburg Times*.

The old veteran had lived next-door to Jefferson Davis. Gillette had joined the Army when he was fifteen years old. Besides being near where the Confederate troops had pierced the Union line during Pickett's Charge, he had also seen Confederate Gen. Stonewall Jackson mortally wounded during the Battle of Chancellorsville in 1863.

Chuck had his picture taken with the man. Gillette still had his hair, though it was white and thinning. He also had a thick white mustache. Chuck asked him to sign his autograph book. Gillette wrote in it he had been at the opening and close of the Battle of Gettysburg.

Gillette invited the Caldwells into his tent and out of the

sun. He sat down on his cot and reached a hand under it. He pulled out a stone jug filled with whiskey.

"Would you like a drink?" Gillette offered George.

George shook his head. "No, thank you."

Gillette shrugged and poured himself a glass and sipped it. Then the trio talked with Chuck eager to ask questions about the war of the weathered veteran. In an old newsreel from the reunion, an interviewer has a conversation with Gillette, which more than likely resembled Chuck's and dozens of others Gillette had during the reunion.

"General Gillette, will you tell us in your own words your experiences during the celebrated Pickett Charge at the Bloody Angle at the Battle of Gettysburg?" the interviewer asks.

"Well, I belonged to the Davis Division, that Davis Brigade and we get about ten feet at the slope, then we had to turn. Those that were living had to turn," Gillette replies.

"What do you mean by *turn*?"

"Run, run like hell."

"You don't mean to say, General Gillette, that soldiers run?"

"Well, if one tells you he didn't, he's telling you a damn lie."

Later in the day, Chuck and his father watched the thirty-unit parade through Gettysburg that ended at the stadium where the Civil War veterans reviewed the modern military men and their equipment. The parade included drum and bugle corps representing the major veteran organizations in the country and many of the states that had troops at the Battle of Gettysburg. Interspersed between the drum and bugle corps were regular Army units representing infantry, tanks, anti-aircraft, field artillery, and cavalry. The other armed forces also had units in the parade. With all of the men and equipment, the parade stretched out for three miles between the reviewing stand at the college and the intersection of Baltimore Pike and Emmitsburg Road. It took two-and-a-half hours for everything in the parade to pass.

The next day was the Caldwells' last full day in Gettysburg. Chuck once again walked through the camps looking for veterans with whom to speak. By the end of the day, he would have nearly fifty autographs from Civil War veterans in his book along with their basic information and picture.

During the afternoon, veterans shook hands across the stone wall at The Angle. The same thing had been done at the 50th-anniversary reunion in 1913, and one couldn't help but notice that there were far fewer veterans around to take part in it in 1938.

The big event of July 3 was the Peace Memorial dedication with its eternal flame, which stood on the hill northwest of the veterans' camp.

President Franklin D. Roosevelt arrived by train at a temporary platform next to the Confederate camp and was escorted in a car to the memorial where over 200,000 people waited.

Chuck and his father were in the crowd not too far away from the monument. The weather was hot, feeling even more so because of the tightly packed bodies. Many people stood for hours waiting to hear the president speak, and at least a half dozen people had to be carried away to get medical care after they collapsed from heat exhaustion.

The president spoke less than ten minutes. Among his comments, he noted, "In later years, new needs arose and with them new tasks, worldwide in their perplexities, their bitterness and their modes of strife. Here in our land, we give thanks that, avoiding war, we seek our ends through the peaceful processes of popular government under the Constitution." He concluded his remarks by accepting the monument on behalf of federal government "in the spirit of brotherhood and peace."

"The Star-Spangled Banner" started playing. Two ropes

reached to the top of the monument and were hidden within a fifty-foot-long American flag. The lines were pulled, and the flag slowly came down to be caught by Union veteran George N. Lockwood, Confederate veteran A. G. Harris, and two regular Army attendants. Lockwood was a ninety-two-year-old Union veteran from Los Angeles, and Harris was a ninety-one-year-old Confederate veteran from McDonough, Georgia. Both men wore the uniforms of their respective armies as they performed their solemn duty.

Following the dedication, the U.S. Army staged a simulated air raid on Gettysburg that included forty-eight aircraft from light attack planes to large bombers. Searchlights on the ground shone up at the planes as they dropped flares.

The military demonstration continued with tank maneuvers by the 66th Infantry Provisional Tank Battalion near Glatfelter Hall on the Gettysburg College campus.

Once night fell, fireworks launched from the crest of Oak Hill.

Chuck fell asleep that night exhausted, but he knew over the past three days he had seen something special and he had been a part of history. That was what he wanted in life.

Note: Charles "Chuck" Caldwell passed away February 7, 2019, in Gettysburg. He was 95 years old.

Next page: Pages from Chuck Caldwell's autograph book from the 75th anniversary of the Battle of Gettysburg. Photo from the author's collection.

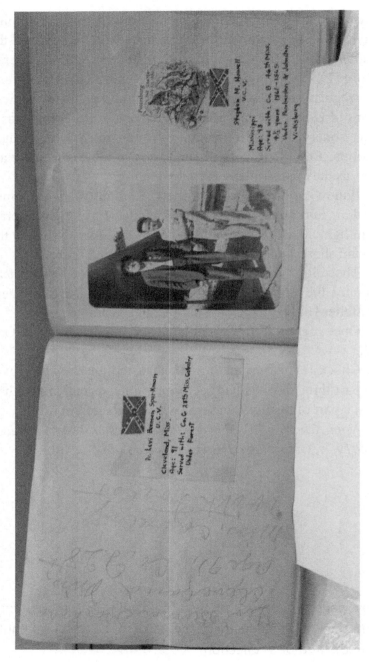

WORLD WARS

Tanks for the Memories

A t the age of 19, Chester Hadley Beymer decided it was time for him to step up and serve his country during World War I. The Los Angeles railroad clerk enlisted in the U.S. Army. His first week in the service was comprised of minimal basic training, paperwork, and physical examinations.

Then he and other raw recruits boarded a train at Point Richmond near San Francisco where they embarked on a six-day cross-country trip to Gettysburg and Camp Colt.

Tanks in War

Though the idea of a tank had been around since Leonardo da Vinci conceived of an armored wagon, the idea of using a tank in war didn't come about until 1903, and then, it still took until 1915 to develop a practical model. With the start of World War I and the United States' entry into the conflict, the U.S. Army looked for a way to integrate tanks into the service.

The Camp with No Name

An unnamed U.S. Army camp was first established on the Gettysburg battlefield in May 1917. The reason it had no name, according to the 1918 Report of the National Military Park Commission, was because "we believe it is the practice when the location is at a conspicuous place on United States land, notably battle fields, such as Gettysburg." The initial location was part of the Codori farm and land where the Round Top branch of the Gettysburg and Harrisburg Railroad was located. The railroad was one reason the army chose the location. It made it easy to move men and equipment directly into and out of the camp.

The camp soon grew as more and more soldiers and supplies were shipped there. Each regiment had 15 or 16 wooden barracks that needed to be constructed. These were not insulated barracks or even fully completed. This temporariness of the construction showed that the camp would not be suitable as a winter quarters for men.

Even though the land where General Pickett had charged would soon be trampled by soldiers once again, the U.S. Army was not ignorant of the historical significance of the park land. In a letter to the Gettysburg Battlefield Commission, the commander of the 61st U.S. Infantry wrote, "…every effort will be made by myself to see that the enlisted men of the 61st infantry do not molest in any way, the monuments, trees, shrubbery, woods, etc. of the Gettysburg National Park."

As the soldiers arrived in camp, three regiments of infantry were housed on the east side of Emmitsburg Road and one regiment was on the west side. An additional regiment was housed on the west side of the road along with a bakery, hospital and motor ambulance pool. Two more regiments were housed near where the Gettysburg Recreation Park is located.

The Army built water and sewer lines to deal with the sanitary issues thousands of men would cause. The number of men at the camp grew to 8,000 at its peak, which was roughly the same population as Gettysburg. The men trained through the summer, but by the end of November only a small detachment of men remained because the camp was not suitable to house soldiers through the cold Pennsylvania winters.

Future president Dwight D. Eisenhower with other officers at Camp Colt. Photo courtesy of the National Park Service.

Camp Colt

The army camp didn't stay deserted for too long. It was re-established on March 6, 1918, with Capt. Dwight Eisenhower commanding. However, this would not be the same camp that had been run in 1917. It would be a training site for America's newest weapon, the tank.

"The Tank Corps was new. There were no precedents except in basic training and I was the only officer in the command. Now I really began to learn about responsibility," Eisenhower wrote *in At Ease: Stories I Tell to Friends.*

Running the camp was Eisenhower's first independent command. He was given the job of training soldiers to run a piece of equipment that hadn't been tested in battle yet and to make matters worse, he had to conduct this training with no tanks.

Beymar said Eisenhower ran an efficient camp. "Discipline was good and there were hardly any gripes to be heard," he wrote.

The practice of not naming camps on battlefields must have ended. The new camp was named for Samuel Colt, the inventor of the Colt Peacemaker, and so Camp Colt was opened. Equipment for tank training was moved from Camp Meade in Maryland to Gettysburg where Camp Colt occupied 176 acres of the Codori farm, 10 acres of the Smith farm and 6 acres of Bryan House place. Much of the current Colt Park housing development was also part of the camp.

The training program Eisenhower developed had soldiers practicing with machine guns mounted on flatbed trucks instead of tanks. They learned to repair engines and to use Morse Code. "At times, HQ entertained English officers who had early war experience with the first English constructed tanks on French battle fields. They came to advise on training. Then again, a few members of Congress would arrive to get a peep at the one and only tin can of a tank which was used for partial training of tankers, especially those small men, who could easily climb into its interior. A 200-pound man just couldn't," recalled George Goshaw in a 1954 *Gettysburg Times* article. He had served at the camp under Eisenhower.

Beymer's group of 99 soldiers quickly realized that their barracks had been horse stables.

"It had been cleaned up and a board floor laid down," Beymer wrote in a letter, which is in the Adams County Historical Society.

114

Empty sacks and blankets sat on the cots. The soldiers had to take the sacks to the building next door to fill them with straw to serve as their mattresses. This was Beymar's home for the next six weeks.

"It was definitely not the Ritz," Beymar wrote. "The plumbing was all outside in the open. One punishment handed out by the Sergeants for most any minor violation was that you and a buddy had the job of picking up three 30 gallon GI cans each morning and carrying them out back and dumping them in to a trench."

Camp Colt was where Beymar's true basic training took place. He had no spare time. He spent his days marching, drilling, marching, learning proper military etiquette, and even more marching.

After basic training, the men were divided into three groups: truck and tank drivers, gunners, and signaling. Beymar was assigned to the latter group. He was trained in hand signaling, light signaling, and Morse Code.

He would practice what he had learned beneath a shade tree near where Pickett's Charge had taken place.

Occasionally the soldiers got day passes that allowed them to visit Gettysburg. Walking back to camp one day with three other soldiers, an officer driving in a roadster with his wife, stopped and told the soldiers to climb aboard.

"We stood on the running boards and sat on the trunk cover," Beymar wrote.

After six weeks, Beymar was assigned to a replacement company that would be sent to Europe to replace soldiers who had died there. About 150 soldiers made up the company.

Each time a call for tankers to join the fighting in Europe came, battalions of men moved to Hoboken, New Jersey, where they boarded transports to Europe. There, they joined the fighting climbing inside real tanks and facing real bullets and mortars.

The camp managed to get two Renault tanks to use by the time that summer arrived. Over the nine months the camp existed more than 9,000 men were trained to fight in the war.

Capt. Dwight Eisenhower with one of Camp Colt's two training tanks. Photo courtesy of the National Park Service.

By October, many of the men had been transferred elsewhere because there were no suitable winter quarters. However, worse than winter happened in the fall of 1918. Spanish Flu swept across the world killing an estimated 60 million people, including 160 at Camp Colt, according to the Gettysburg *Star and Sentinel*. During the month, the bodies literally piled up. The dead soldiers were taken to the Grand Army of the Republic Hall in town until arrangements could be made to ship their bodies home. As each body was taken to the depot, soldiers gave it a military escort through Gettysburg.

"The infirmary was swamped and tents were set up on the parade ground and cots installed to take care of the overflow," Beymar wrote. "These were the newest and less serious patients."

SECRETS OF THE GETTYSBURG BATTLEFIELD

The soldiers who weren't sick became nurse's aides and cared for the sick. Beymar had the night shift and cared for one tent filled with eight sick soldiers. He mainly brought them water and helped them to the bathroom.

"It was raining, and the sick ones died like flies," Beymar wrote. "The truck took pine boxes to the railroad express station every day."

Surprisingly, Beymar didn't fall ill nor did most of his fellow California recruits. Of the 99 recruits who came east with Beymar, only one man fell ill and he died. Eventually, 160 soldiers at Camp Colt died from Spanish Flu in the fall of 1918.

Closing the Camp

As the flu abated, so did the war. The Allies and Germans signed the armistice ending World War I on November 11, 1918. "When November 11th came upon us, Ike and his entire staff were saddened, knowing full well that they were cheated out of actual battle service," Goshaw recalled. "From then on, there was a let down on training and the necessary daily duties."

Beymar left the camp on October 18. He served in the American Expeditionary Force in France until March 18, 1919. He was discharged from the army at San Francisco on April 21, 1919.

The orders to close Camp Colt came on November 17. Then remaining men were sent to Camp Dix in New Jersey for their final discharge.

Veterans of the camp soon organized reunions in Gettysburg, although there was no longer a camp to visit. The first reunion in the 1940's was marked with the planting of the large pine tree on the east side of Emmitsburg Road south of the entrance to the old visitor's center. The former soldiers of

Camp Colt planted the tree in remembrance of the tankers' fallen comrades. You can still see it today along with a commemorative plaque summarizing the history of Camp Colt.

Camp Colt as seen from the Old Emmitsburg Road. Photo courtesy of the National Park Service.

The Marines Who Fought at Gettysburg

T he U.S. Marines fought valiantly in World War I in places like the Battle of Belleau Wood in France. After the deadly fighting there to drive the entrenched German troops from Belleau Wood, Army Gen. John J. Pershing, commander of the American Expeditionary Force, said, "The deadliest weapon in the world is a Marine and his rifle."

However, that didn't stop Pershing and others from wanting to disband the Marine Corps after the war was won.

Maj. Gen. John A. Lejeune understood that his Marine Corps needed to fight for survival in the political arena just as hard as they fought on the battlefield. After WWI as the politicians spoke about disbanding the Marines, Lejeune devised a campaign to raise public awareness about the Marine Corps.

One way he did this was instead of going to obscure places to conduct war games and train, he took the Marines to iconic locations and put the men out in front of the public. The U.S. War Department still controlled the national military parks, such as Gettysburg, which meant the Marines could use the parks as a training ground. Lejeune did just that with a series of annual training exercises, which started in 1921 with a re-enactment of the Battle of the Wilderness.

Early in the morning of Monday, June 19, 1922, over 5,000 Marines at the Marine Camp Quantico – more than a quarter of the Corps – marched onto waiting barges supplied by the U.S. Navy. At 4 a.m., four Navy tug boats towed eight large barges up the Potomac River toward Washington, D.C. Meanwhile, tanks and trucks towing artillery pieces rolled out along the Richmond Road headed for the same destination.

Camp Harding housed over 5,000 Marines on the Gettysburg Battlefield in 1922. Photo courtesy of the U.S. Marine Corps Historical Company.

The march involved the entire 5th and 6th Regiments, a squadron of the 1st Marine Air Wing, and elements of the 10th Marine Artillery. *The (Baltimore) Sun* noted that these Marines were ready for anything and had cleaned out Quantico of anything they could move. "The 5,000 men are carrying the equipment of a complete division of nearly 20,000. In the machine-gun outfits especially the personnel is skeletonized, while the material is complete. Companies of 88 men are carrying ammunition, range finders and other technical gear for companies of about 140."

The Marines spent their first night at East Potomac Park, south of the Washington Monument. Once they had fully set up camp, they marched past the White House where President Warren G. Harding and other dignitaries reviewed them.

"Observers declared that this is the first time that troops have passed in review through the White House grounds since the Civil War," the *Marine Corps Gazette* reported.

It took a half an hour for the Marines to pass in front of the president as the 134-piece combined Marine bands played music.

On June 20, the Marines marched to Bethesda, Md. The following day they marched to Gaithersburg, Md., where they spent two nights. On June 23, they marched to Ridgeville, Md. Then the next day, it was Frederick, Md. They spent the final night of the march on a farm just north of Thurmont, Md.

All along the way, the Marines drew crowds that watched them march past. They also invited visitors into their camps to hear the band play or to talk with the Marines. Occasionally, they played baseball against local teams, and they always sought any living Civil War veterans to invite them to come to Gettysburg and watch the re-enactments as a guest of the Marines.

Many of the Marines were heroes who had served in Europe during World War I and they didn't spend a lot of time talking about their overseas adventures.

Camp Harding, named for the president, was set up on the Codori Farm and just north of the North Carolina Monument, and near the McMillan farmhouse near the farm and park boundary. Various newspapers reported the size of the encampment to be from 65 to 100 acres. GySgt. Thomas E. Williams, director of the United States Marine Corps Historical Company, stated that 100 acres is closer to the actual size of the encampment.

Although the War Department controlled the parks, it did not want to damage a historic sites. This resulted in a command decision to restrict any heavy vehicles and vehicles hauling heavy loads, to access the camp via Emmitsburg Road, while light vehicles and vehicles carrying lighter loads could travel up West Confederate Avenue.

Because of the planned stay of President Harding and his wife, Florence, in the camp for a night, the Marines erected a structure for the couple and their guests.

The site chosen was a relatively high point of the field along West Confederate Avenue, just north of the North Carolina Monument, and was near the McMillan farmhouse near the farm and park boundary.

The Gettysburg Times described the presidential compound this way:

"The floor plan of the large structure is of a unique design, being semi-circular in shape...In the center of the building is the President's public reception room, which is 40 feet in length by 25 feet in width...on either side of the public reception room are large rooms to be used as combination sitting rooms and bed rooms, the one, on the left...being allocated to the president and his wife, while the one on the right will be used by (presidential) Secretary George Christian...In the rear of each of these rooms are private baths, completely finished with all the fittings of a modern bath and the added convenience of hot and cold water."

The Canvas White House was "officially" completed on June 29 with the installation of six porcelain bathtubs. Martin

MBT twin-engine bomber/torpedo planes "strapped" with the bathtubs flew to Camp Harding. The Marines took this precaution to avoid damaging the heavy porcelain bathtubs, which might have happened during overland transport. "These are the first bathtubs ever carried by airplane, it is believed," according to the *Gettysburg Times*.

The Canvas White House where President Warren G. Harding, his wife, and guests stayed on the Gettysburg Battlefield. Photo courtesy of the U.S. Marine Corps Historical Company.

As part of the week-long training and military demonstrations to be held on the Gettysburg battlefield, much of the Marine 1st Aviation Group, including de Havilland DH-4Bs, which served as a light bomber, fighter, and observation craft,

Vought VE-7 training and observation planes, Martin MBT bomber/torpedo planes, and two Type-F kite observation balloons, was dispatched to Camp Harding to participate. All of these planes were of the bi-wing type. The kite balloons were inflated with highly-explosive hydrogen, and tethered to the ground via cables.

Capt. George Hamilton, in command of a squadron of fighters providing "scout duty" while escorting the Marine infantry, along with GySgt. George Martin, were flying a DH-4B fighter as they left their encampment at Thurmont shortly after noon on July 26 and proceeded north.

His De Havilland flew at the rear of a formation of four planes serving as air scouts for the Marines marching from Thurmont to Gettysburg. No one noticed anything wrong with the planes in the squadron until the flights began to approach the landing site at Camp Harding. Two of the planes in the escort landed safely in a designated portion of the fields near the intersection of Long Lane and Emmitsburg Road.

Then Hamilton and Martin's plane suddenly went into a nose dive from about 3,000 feet up. It became a tail spin. The plane crashed on the William Johns farm around 1:05 p.m., near what is now the intersection of Johns Avenue and Culp Street in the Colt Park development. *The Star and Sentinel* reported the impact occurred within 50 feet of tents and equestrian equipment belonging to the Lew Dufour Carnival, which had set-up along Steinwehr Avenue.

Hamilton died at the scene and Martin died a short time later at Warner Hospital.

The accident is believed to have been due to the difference in the altimeter's reading at Quantico and at Gettysburg. Quantico is on sea level, while Gettysburg is 600 feet above sea level. When the altimeter reads 1,000 feet at the latter place, the actual distance is only 400 feet.

Hamilton and Martin were killed in the line-of-duty in the service of their country, and the deaths of the two Marines are presently the only known military line-of-duty deaths that have occurred on the Gettysburg battlefield since 1863.

Marine officers stated that they believed Hamilton tried his best to avoid the crowds at the carnival, knowing his plane was in trouble. The aircraft could have struck the carnival itself if he had continued to try and maneuver the plane out of its plunge toward the earth, and possibly kill many people in the resulting crash.

The bulk of the Marines arrived in camp on June 26. The then began military exercises and learning more about the historical context of how the Battle of Gettysburg proceeded.

As part of the training exercises, officers planned spontaneous engagements to which various Marine units had to react, and were to occur at any time. The idea behind the scramble-into-action concept was to provide command, control, and deployment challenges while in hostile territory.

They had to do much of this training in the rain, which was sometimes torrential, and soon turned Camp Harding into a mud bog.

President Harding and his party arrived around 4 p.m. on Saturday, July 1. Among the presidential party were the First Lady Florence Harding, Gen. John "Blackjack" Pershing, Charles G. Dawes who was the retiring director of the budget, Brig. Gen. Charles Sawyer who served as the president's personal physician, and the president's personal secretary, George Christian.

The President inspected the camp and was then escorted out to watch the Pickett's Charge re-enactment from the Ziegler Grove observation tower, which lasted less than an hour.

Pennsylvania Governor William Sproul, Virginia Governor Elbert Trinkle, Acting Secretary of the Navy Theodore

Roosevelt, Jr., U.S. Senator George Wharton Pepper (Pa.), Commandant of the Marine Corps Maj. Gen. John A. Lejeune, Maj. Gen. Wendell C. Neville, Brig. Gen. Smedley Butler, Christian, U.S. Senator Joseph Medill McCormick (Ill.), Speaker of the House Frederick H. Gillett were some of the other guests. Many foreign governments sent representatives to watch the re-enactments as well.

Planes of the U.S. Marines 1st Aviation Group parked on the battlefield in 1922. Photo courtesy of the U.S. Marine Corps Historical Company.

The first day of the three-day presentation of Pickett's Charge, July 1, opened with torrential rain and thunderstorms. By early afternoon, it became oppressive heat.

The quartermaster supplied a half bushel of beets to each regiment to cut up and boil to simulate blood. The troops were also issued bandages to apply to the "wounds."

As the time of battle approached, an estimated 100,000 spectators descended upon the scene.

Suddenly, two of the Confederate 75mm guns fired, the

signal for Lieutenant Campbell to commence the opening artillery barrage he had ordered "concealed" in an artillery park on Seminary Ridge (Several 75mm guns were also placed along Cemetery Ridge and around Little Round Top to represent the federal artillery), George M. Chandler wrote in the July 1922 *Infantry Journal.*

U.S. Marines relax in Camp Harding. Photo courtesy of the U.S. Marine Corps Historical Company.

When the half-hour barrage subsided, the Marines representing the Southern advance began, preceded by a skirmish line of sharpshooters. The advancing Confederates bore flags marked in such a manner that the spectators knew whose troops they were representing from the original battle. Confederate regiments carried white and red Army signal flags as their respective battle flags, while the names of the generals represented in the charge were written in white on blue cloth.

At first, there was so much smoke on the field that the advancing Confederate battle line spectators could not see the Confederates. When people did see the soldiers in the haze, some said it appeared the ghosts of soldiers past had returned out of time itself and onto the battlefield.

Writing about the ensuing fight, the *New York Tribune* said, "Then they began to move forward...and for the watchers there was a thrill as though the ghosts of Pickett's men were massed once more for another try for victory...there were six lines of men stretching along a mile front."

Some of the advancing troops had also been provided with shotguns loaded with black powder rounds they would fire towards the ground, as the troops progressed to simulate artillery shell explosions. The Marines in the vicinity of the "explosions" would then fall "dead" or "wounded" around the detonation thus produced.

Standing at the base of the Ziegler's Grove tower, Park Superintendent Cope, emotionally caught up in the moment he had once lived through, mounted the first step of the tower and yelled at the advancing Confederates, "Get back there, you Rebs!"

The Marines, having crossed the Emmitsburg Road, continued on toward the stone wall that comprised the high water mark of the Battle of Gettysburg, at the crest of Cemetery Ridge, but not before a portion of the advancing Marines charged the Codori homestead on the east side of the road, routing an army of chickens – literally, in this case.

At 5:20 p.m., the climactic storming of "The Angle" began. As the final moments approached, *The Sun* reported, "The din of firing was fearful. From the far-off woods on Seminary ridge the cannonade had almost ceased, but from all around...the Union guns now roared a thunderous chorus. Then came the 'rebel yell' and the last rush. They were at the stone fence, in a yelling, shooting mass. The Confederates were at the Bloody Angle again."

The President and his party left the next morning, but the Marines' exercises continued on July 3-4. On July 4, the Civil War was updated with airplanes, howitzers, hydrogen-filled observation balloons, tanks, machine guns, anti-aircraft guns, "Big Ear" monitoring devices, radio communications, and mortars.

Capt. George Hamilton (left) and GySgt. George Martin (right). A a plane accident on the Gettysburg Battlefield in 1922 killed both Marines. Photos courtesy of the U.S. Marine Corps Historical Company and the Buffalo Evening News.

That morning, an observation balloon ascended to about 2,000 feet above the Marine camp, representing Confederate observation craft. As soon as the balloons were aloft, their artillery which was posted on Seminary Ridge fired, the purpose of the balloons being to ascertain the effect of the rounds being aimed at the enemy positions.

A squadron of four enemy planes, representing Union aircraft, appeared above Cemetery Ridge to defend the forces located there, and just as quickly, two squadrons of fighters representing the Southern forces rushed up and towards the enemy planes, and were soon engaged in dogfighting, "in which nose dives, spins, loops, Immelman turns and other war maneuvers of fighting aircraft succeeded each other in rapid succession, while bursts of machine gun fire from aloft told when a pilot has succeeded in securing a deadly position on the tail of some other craft," the *New York Tribune* reported.

One of the enemy (Union) planes suddenly broke off and dove at the targeted observation balloon. "Speeding like an angry wasp straight at the big 'sausage,' it veered away and circled the balloon with a 'tat-tat-tat' of machine gun fire. Then it headed back to join its fellows," *The Sun* wrote.

The assault on the balloon was brief, but fatal. Licks of flame appeared, then spread rapidly throughout the craft, which had been inflated with a "half-million cubic feet of hydrogen gas." A dummy, it was generally reported, wearing a parachute was cast forth from the observation basket attached to the underside of the balloon, while a second figure fell to the earth without a chute. As the burning balloon fell to the earth somewhere on the west side of Seminary Ridge, along with the slowly descending "parachutist," the crowd was stunned, some believing the figures were actually people, and that one of them had fallen to certain death. There's a couple versions of what happened, but the one that fits the facts is that a Marine on the balloon ignited it and threw a dummy out and then followed wearing a parachute.

Marine trucks hauled much of the equipment from Quantico, Va., to Camp Harding. Photo courtesy of the U.S. Marine Corps Historical Company.

With the balloon down, the fighting began. A smokescreen using smoke candles was laid-down on the field before the Confederate advance, and around 10:40 a.m., the Marines began their assault. Unlike the reenactments of July 1 and 3, the Confederates attacked the Union position as they would have done in a "modern" engagement, in squads and platoons, rather than in long shoulder-to-shoulder firing lines.

"The machine guns were really there yesterday (July 4). They were firing real bullets. Machine guns can't fire blank ammunition. So were all the other machine guns in the woods on Seminary Ridge. But pits had been dug all around them and the bullets were diving harmlessly into the earth," *The Sun* reported. Further confirming this, the *Washington Post* noted that "the machine guns used ball ammunition, for machine guns will not function with blank ammunition. The guns were emplaced in previously prepared pits, and the stream of steel-jacketed lead was pumped into the soggy earth."

As the battle approached a climactic conclusion, the Confederates seemed to run into some stiff opposition in and around the Codori house and farm buildings, which neither small-arms fire, machine-gun fire, nor light artillery fire could clear out, resulting in the troops who were attempting to cap-

131

ture that position calling for armor support to help.

Four M1917 tanks rolled into action. "The tanks went sneeringly up to the Codori house, around the barn, around to the back door, through the chicken yards, up the front porch, firing explosive shells (supposedly) through the windows," *The Sun* stated. "In a few moments they waddled away, and you could almost imagine them chuckling horribly, heading again toward the rear to sleep and snore until there was no more killing to do. The enemy in the Codori House was silenced forever."

Marines recreate the Battle of Gettysburg on the battlefield in 1922. Photo courtesy of the U.S. Marine Corps Historical Company.

One tank involved at the Codori house became a "causality" in the attack, enemy fire took it out of action.

Photo from the 1922 Marine maneuvers in Gettysburg with simulated casualties. Photos courtesy of the U.S. Marine Corps Historical Company.

The Marines broke down Camp Harding on July 5. The return march to Quantico began on Thursday morning, July 6 at 6 a.m. It retraced the same route they had taken from Quantico to Gettysburg except for one difference. Instead of spending one night in Frederick and two nights in Rockville, the Marines spent two nights in Frederick and a single night in Rockville.

In Frederick, the Marines received a special visitor as President Harding and his party stopped by on their way back from Marion, Ohio. The Hardings' car stopped outside the camp and the president and his wife stood in the road as the Expeditionary Force Marine Corps Band serenaded them.

Marines recreate the Battle of Gettysburg during the 1922 Marine maneuvers in Gettysburg. Photos courtesy of the U.S. Marine Corps Historical Company.

When Gettysburg Reached for the Sky

W hen World War II started in 1939, the United States had roughly 38,000 trained pilots. It wasn't enough to fight a war. Men were willing to join the Army Air Corps, but there weren't enough instructors to train them all.

Often the men waiting to become pilots were members of the Army Enlisted Reserve. "This Enlisted Reserve consisted of young men who had been picked by the Air Corps after a suitable examination but who had been permitted to stay temporarily in civilian life pending vacancies in the various Air Corps training centers," the Gettysburg College *Alumni News* reported.

As the number of pilots increased, it became clear that the best ones were those who had studied subjects pertinent to flying, such as mathematics, physics, and advanced geography, while in college. However, fewer and fewer of the Air Corps openings were being filled by college students.

At the same time, many small colleges felt financial strain as their students joined the military and left college. Some colleges even considered closing because of lagging enrollment, according to the *Alumni News*.

Then someone realized colleges could be helped and the quality of the pilot candidates improved at the same time. The Enlisted Reserve men would undergo intensive training to pre-

135

pare them to become pilots at colleges around the country that had classroom space. The *Alumni News* estimated that the program would pack twice as much education into the same time as a regular college program.

"Thus, then, these institutions could stay open and retain their financial solvency, and the Army Air Forces could get their men trained along exactly the lines that were desired. One other factor which has been somewhat overlooked in regards to the training program, is that that thousands of young men who would normally not go to college had the opportunity of getting a rather good college education and in the collegiate surroundings which mean almost more than the book-work itself," the *Alumni News* reported.

Gettysburg College was chosen as one institution where pilots would be trained and in the fall of 1942, the Civilian Pilot Training School opened in Gettysburg. Young men received classroom training at Gettysburg College and flying and mechanical instruction at the new Gettysburg Airport on Mummasburg Road.

"It is now possible for an American boy to start from scratch on a flying career and become an Army pilot instructor in 32 weeks," Richard Bircher told a meeting of the Gettysburg Lions Club in 1942. He was given charge of both the Civilian Pilot Training program and the airport.

Gettysburg College was one of the few colleges in the country that offered all four Civilian Pilot Training Courses – Elementary, Secondary, Cross-Country, and Instructor. The college also had the largest quota of students assigned to any one school operator, according to *The Gettysburg Times*.

"We believe we are doing a worthwhile service in the war effort by training the men who will instruct Army and Navy cadet pilots in the service flying schools," Bircher said.

The Army Air Corps and the colleges ran these initial

programs, but the Army Air Corps soon took over the entire program. Rather than training the young men while they were waiting to enter the military, the Army trained Air Corps enlistees after they had already gone through basic training. By mid-March 1943, the CPT program transitioned into the Army program in Gettysburg.

The old airport on Mummasburg Road. Photo courtesy of Musselman Library Special Collections and Archives.

During its short service, the CPT program trained 84 men, each of whom had received 35 hours of flying instruction and 240 of ground school training. Besides providing practical experience, the *Alumni News* reported that the flying time, "also serves the double purpose of giving the classification center and us an insight into whether or not the student is basically unfitted to become a pilot, and whether or not the student has a fear of heights, or is subject to airsickness."

The Army Air Corps continued to train pilots at Gettysburg. An Army quartermaster worked with the college personnel to arrange for food, classroom space, and sleeping quarters for the training pilots. Additional plumbing even had to the run at the college, according to the *Alumni News*.

The arriving students had completed their basic training and were ready for specialized training at the college.

"Some of these Air Crew members or students had had some university experience and, naturally, did not require all of the basic subjects that were being taught to their fellow students, and also in many cases did not require the full five months academic schedule. These more advanced aircrew students did not have to take the full five months' course," the *Alumni News* reported. The need for pilots was too great to leave pilots relearning what they already knew.

Once the program was up and running, the *Alumni News* reported that 85 percent of all Gettysburg College's male students were enrolled in the reserves and totaled nearly 300 young men. In addition, this did not include students who have reserved in the advance Reserve Officers Training Corps. This was about 100 additional young men.

Besides, learning to fly, the students took classes in meteorology, navigation, air-engine operations, flight theory, aircraft, aircraft identification, military science and courtesy, military and physical training, code, military force organization.

This push for pilots succeeded. By the end of 1942, roughly 200,000 men in the United States were pilots.

German POWs Stay on the Battlefield During WWII

G unter Habock was imprisoned in Gettysburg, but rather than considering it a trial, he enjoyed his time here as a prisoner. It was so enjoyable, in fact, that he returned to Gettysburg in 1970 to show his wife and son where he had spent part of World War II.

"He was a boy of 15 in 1939 when Hitler's Brown Shirts demonstrated for possession of the Polish Corridor and remembers the Polish army in the city," *The Gettysburg Times* reported.

An 18-year-old Habock was in Danzig in 1943, studying architecture when the German Army draften him.

Habock initially served as a paratrooper in the German army, but he transferred to infantry when the Germans lost all of their planes at St. Lo, Normandy, after the Allies strafed the location. He was sent to fight in July 12, 1944, and captured along with 24 other paratroopers on July 28.

The American soldiers took the captured Germans to Le Havre, where 42 ships waited to sail to the U.S. These ships were loaded with 2,000 German prisoners.

The ships docked at New York and the prisoners were off loaded onto trains to be transported to various prisoner of war camps in the U.S. Several hundred were put on a train to Carlisle. At Carlisle, trucks waited to take about 100 of the prisoners to Gettysburg.

Gettysburg housed German prisoners of war from May 31, 1944, until February 1945. It was one of hundreds of POW camps throughout the country during the war.

On May 31, 1944, fifty prisoners of war were transferred from Camp Meade in Maryland to Gettysburg. The U. S. War Department set up hundreds of POW camps throughout the country during the war. Similar camps could also be found nearby in Frederick, Md., and Pine Grove Furnace Park.

However, when the prisoners arrived in Gettysburg, there was no camp in which to house them. The POWs were set to work building a 400-foot by 600-foot stockade surrounding the camp along Emmitsburg Road next to the old Home Sweet Home Motel. During this construction phase, the prisoners were housed at the National Guard Armory on Confederate Avenue.

Three days after the first arrival of prisoners, another 100 joined them and then an additional 350 came a week later.

The tent camp was ready for occupancy on June 20, 1944. The POWs moved into the new camp and 425 of them worked at local farms helping with the pea harvest.

Pea farmers weren't the only ones who could get prison laborers. All a farmer had to do was apply to the employment service in Gettysburg.

"Use of German prisoners of war in Adams county's canneries and orchards during the last two years allowed the production of thousands of dollars worth of food that otherwise would not have been processed, E. A. Crouse, head of the local USES office, said today in releasing figures on the amount of work performed by the POWS," the *Gettysburg Times* reported in 1946.

Prison labor wasn't used to replace the existing labor force in the county but to supplement it. Civilians were always given first preference at the work, but there wasn't always enough interest in filling the jobs. Crouse noted in one instance that 5,000 letters had been mailed asking for workers to help cut pulpwood. Only 15 replies were received.

Even with a need for the workers, the *Gettysburg Times* noted, "Some canners and others refused to have anything to do with the former enemy troops and some employe(e)e who would have had to work beside the Germans refused to do so."

However, need outweighed distaste, and POWs worked alongside civilians. This helped break down some of the prejudice against the prisoners as the civilians realized things they had in common rather than the differences between them.

For their efforts, the prisoners received 80 cents a day. Their remaining daily earnings, which was usually between 50 and 60 cents an hour, was sent to the federal government. According to the National Park Service, the federal government received $138,000 from the Gettysburg POW camp from June 8 through November 1, 1944. On days that a prisoner didn't work, he received 10 cents a day. The prisoners were paid in coupons, which they could use as cash in the camp exchange.

Besides peas, the prisoners helped with cherry and apple harvests. The Gettysburg POWs were sent with a guard detail to work in nearby canneries, lumber mills and farms.

"I ran the cider press and drank lots of apple juice!" Habock told *The Gettysburg Times*.

Later, he would work at a fertilizer plant in York and loading pulpwood onto trucks and railroad cars in Ortanna.

As the harvests ended and winter approached, temperatures fell. Many of the prisoners were moved to Camp Sharpe (the former Camp Colt). After Camp Colt had closed at the end of World War I, Civilian Conservation Corps workers had used the barracks during the Great Depression era. The Army refurbished the barracks and put them back into military use as Camp Sharpe.

Camp Sharpe in Gettysburg housed German POWs. Photo courtesy of the Adams County Historical Society.

Though the prisoners were generally docile, there were some problems. One prisoner hanged himself in an Aspers cannery. Two other prisoners escaped but were recaptured eight days later. The prisoners even tried to unsuccessfully strike a couple times.

Capt. Laurence Thomas, a former school superintendent, commanded the camp. He also managed the camp at nearby

Pine Grove Furnace. He was a good choice because he could speak German and could communicate with the prisoners and diffuse a lot of issues before they became problems.

Many times, this simply involved separating the hardcore Nazi and SS soldiers from the common soldiers. Most of the soldiers simply wanted to get through the war and realized that the conditions in the American camps, which followed the Geneva Convention, were not harsh.

Camp Sharpe closed in February 1945, though a skeleton crew of soldiers remained for another year to close down the camp. At its peak in July 1944, the Gettysburg POW camp held 932 prisoners of war, some of whom returned after the war to visit Gettysburg as guests.

Habock left Camp Sharpe in February 1946 and was sent to Indiantown Gap, Pa., then to Ft. Meade, Md., and finally to Camp Shank, N.Y. From there, he was returned to LaHavre in June 1946 and discharged in Babenhausin, Germany.

He returned to his hometown of Danzig, but found that the Russians had expelled all Germans from it so he and his family had to be moved to Hanover, Germany.

He earned his degree and became a contractor building apartments and homes. They married in 1947 and had three children.

The Habocks flew into Ontario on vacation and visited Niagara Falls before visiting the sites where Habock had been as prisoner.

"They visited the Peach Glen plant today, where Habock found many changes," the *Gettysburg Times* reported.

While in Gettysburg, he met with Eugene Clapper who had also been captured at St. Lo. However, the Germans captured Clapper and sent him to a German POW camp. As the two compared notes on their POW experiences, Habock told

Clapper, "It was much worse for you than for me. I had enough to eat and the work was not like that."

At its peak in July 1944, the Gettysburg POW camp held 932 prisoners of war, some of whom, like Habock returned after the war to visit Gettysburg as guests.

Gettysburg Maps Used in WWII

A t the end of World War II, it was decided that Japanese Emperor Hirohito's personal fortune would pay part of the reparations bills incurred by the Allies during the war. Russell Brines, reporting for the Associated Press, wrote that the decision "is apt to become the biggest political and social bombshell yet involving the already harried monarch."

The Emperor's worth on paper was more than $106 million, of which $22.4 million were liquid assets. Even his entire fortune would have been "a mere drop in the reparations bucket at best," according to *The Gettysburg Times*.

The move was considered an indictment that the Emperor was, in part, responsible for the war. In particular, it was assumed that the Japanese people would feel that the action was indirectly labeling Hirohito a war criminal.

Special American detectives were sent into Japan to catalog the Emperor's holdings and search for any hidden money, accounts, or items of value. During their search, they "unearthed nearly two tons of secret Japanese military maps including many on Alaska, and one set of carefully segregated Civil war Gettysburg battle maps," the newspaper reported.

No explanation was ever given where the maps came from or what they were used for.

It seems likely that the maps were used to study the strategies and maneuvers used by both Union and Confederate generals during the war.

How the maps came to be in possession of the Emperor and Japanese government, they may have come from when Japanese emissaries attended the Marine re-enactments of Pickett's Charge in 1922.

Navy officers study maps of the Pacific Theater. Photo courtesy of the U.S. Navy.

One quarter of the U.S. Marine Corps marched from Quantico, Va., to Gettysburg that summer to conduct both historical and modern versions of Pickett's Charge. About 100,000 people, including President Warren G. Harding, attended the event. In addition, there were many military representatives in attendance, including those from foreign countries.

Representing Japan were Capt. Osami Nagano, attaché from the Japanese Navy, Commander M. Hibine, assistant attaché from the Japanese Navy, Maj. Gen. H. Haraguchi, Japanese military attaché, Capt. Y. Fujii, assistant Japanese military attaché, and Capt. K. Matsumoto, assistant Japanese military attaché.

Nagano eventually became the Japanese Combined Fleet Commander-in-chief in 1937.

"Nineteen years after standing on the fields of Gettysburg observing the Marine assaults, Nagano met with Emperor Hirohito on November 3, 1941, and that meeting resulted in Hirohito authorizing Nagano on November 5 to give the go-ahead to an act that would become known as "a day that will live in infamy" – the attack on Pearl Harbor, December 7, 1941," Richard D. L. Fulton and myself wrote in our book, *The Last to Fall: The 1922 March, Battles, & Deaths of U.S. Marines at Gettysburg.*

This was not the only way that maps connected with Gettysburg were used during WWII. The Navy had a war mapping program that ran out of the Lee-Meade Inn on Emmitsburg Road during the war. *The Gettysburg Times* reported that, "only a few of the top men there knew that charts needed by the U. S. Hydrographic office to complete highly detailed maps for the invasion—and later the occupation—of Japan, most of the charts for the bloody Iwo Jima campaign and scores of other Yankee targets in the Pacific were being made there."

Beginning in 1943, around 45 men with the U.S. Forestry Service were employed in the work. The work done in Gettysburg led to new mapmaking methods and the development of new equipment for the creation of maps. The National Park Service employed civilian guards to protect the inn around the clock and when the maps weren't being worked on, they were stored in a special vault in the inn's basement.

The maps turned out to be so accurate and useful, that Admiral Chester Nimitz sent a letter to the group praising their work.

Aerial photos were sent to the inn from the Pacific Theater. Once in Gettysburg, the photos were used to develop the maps under secrecy.

Locals Aid POWs
in Their Escape

B y 1946, World WarII may have been over, but that
didn't mean the U.S. Army had repatriated all of the
prisoners held in American POW camps. That was
an ongoing process that some prisoners didn't want to wait
for.

Two German prisoners held at the old Civilian Conservation Corps camp on the Gettysburg battlefield escaped on
January 3, 1946. "The men are said to have escaped through
the stockade fence at an unguarded corner about 8 o'clock
Thursday," the *Gettysburg Times* reported. The camp used
refurbished barracks from Camp Colt.

Their absence was noted late in the evening, but it wasn't
until the following morning that word went out to Pennsylvania State Police substation that the men had escaped. Capt.
C. M. Morfit, the officer in charge of the camp, refused to
give out any further information.

What information the *Gettysburg Times* reporters gathered came from the public relations officer at Indiantown
Gap. Pa. The two escapees were 20-year-old Hans Harloff
who had been captured in June 1944, and 24-year-old Ber-
nard Wagner who had been captured in May 1943.

After four days on the run, the prisoners were recaptured
on Jan. 7 near Zora. "Acting on a tip the authorities found the

pair hidden in a straw stack adjacent to an unused barn on the property of Clayton Phillips," according to the newspaper.

A group of camp guards, state police officers, and an FBI agent captured the Germans, who offered no resistance. One officer present at the capture said the prisoners were "very scared."

FBI Agent H. B. Fletcher interviewed the prisoners and reported later that they had escaped because "they liked America, wanted to see more of it and hoped to reach a large city and stay in this country rather than return to Germany." While this may have been true, Harloff had another reason for escaping that he didn't share with the authorities.

Harloff could speak English, but Wagner's command of the language was limited. The Germans told the FBI agent they were hungry and hadn't eaten in two days. They also said they had walked from the camp to Zora, reaching it on Saturday night or early Sunday morning. They had had no particular destination in mind. This turned out to be a lie.

The men were not punished since the war had ended, but they were returned to the camp.

The authorities continued investigating some apparent inconsistencies in the Germans' story. This lead to the indictment of Byron J. Cease, 44; his wife Lovell, 37; and their daughter Pearl, 19. The lived in Orrtanna, and the women worked at a canning factory there.

Harloff had met the women while he worked at the factory during the summer of 1945 on work release. For their efforts, the prisoners received 80 cents a day. The remaining amount of their daily earnings, which was usually between 50 and 60 cents an hour, was sent to the federal government. The prisoners weren't supposed to fraternize with other workers, but Harloff was apparently smitten by Pearl.

He wrote her a note in English saying he wanted to meet

her. "Other notes followed and finally the German told the girl he was going to escape to be with her. She warned him against the attempt and asked him to go back to Germany and then return to this country for her," the *Gettysburg Times* reported.

After Harloff and Wagner escaped on Jan. 3, they arrived at the farm the following day. The Ceases gave them food and clothing and allowed them to stay the night on a vacant property near the Cease property.

The following day, Byron took the Germans to another abandoned property near Zora. This was where the authorities recaptured them on Jan. 7.

A federal grand jury in Scranton, Pa., indicted the Ceases for aiding in the prisoners' escape later in March. The maximum penalty for the charges was $10,000 and 10 years in prison.

The case went to trial in May in Harrisburg, Pa. The Ceases pleaded guilty to harboring escaped prisoners. At one point, the judge read two letters that Pearl had written to Harloff in open court. "As he read the letters the girl sobbed. Her father took a handkerchief from his pocket and wiped her eyes," the newspaper reported.

Judge Albert Watson considered the case and gave the family suspended sentences of a year and a day. He placed the parents on one-year probation and Pearl on a two-year probation.

"Judge Watson said that since the war was over when the escape was made a period of imprisonment would serve no good purpose in view of the good reputation borne by the family in Adams county," the *Gettysburg Times* reported.

Vandals Nearly Kill the Eisenhower Tree

I t was dedicated as an act of admiration and unity from all 48 states and two territories, but one act of violence nearly destroyed it.

At the end of August 1954, around 300 former tankers returned to their old training ground for a two-day reunion. The event included a parade and speakers, but it culminated with the planting of a 25-foot-tall northern pine on the Gettysburg Battlefield along Emmitsburg Road.

This memorial was unique. It was a living memorial among hundreds of stone sentinels. It was a memorial to Camp Colt and not the Civil War, and it was planted in soil from all 48 states, plus Alaska and Hawaii, which were territories.

Each state sent a pound of soil from a significant historical site within its borders so that the tree would be nourished in "earth steeped in the blood of American soldiers from the Revolution through the great wars of our republic," according to the *Gettysburg Times*.

During the tree planting ceremony, Lt. Gen. Floyd L. Parks conducted the ceremony for a crowd of 3,000 people. Thomas White, national adjutant of the Tank Corps Association read a roll of states and described where their soil contribution came from. The contributions included:

- Georgia sent soil from beneath the treads of a tank in

the armored units of Camp Stewart.

- South Carolina sent soil from the Kings Mountain Battlefield.
- Texas sent soil from the Alamo.
- Louisiana sent soil from the Chalmette Battlefield, where part of the Battle of New Orleans had been fought.
- North Dakota sent soil from Fort Lincoln where Gen. Custer and his 7th Cavalry had set out from to fight their ill-fated battle.
- Massachusetts' soil came from the home of Gen. George Patton.
- Vermont's soil came from the homestead of President Calvin Coolidge.
- Colorado sent earth from the home of President Dwight Eisenhower's mother.
- Kentucky's soil came from Fort Knox.
- Florida's soil came from beneath a cannon outside of the courthouse in historic Jacksonville.

The *Gettysburg Times* noted, "Few shrines in America will be so deeply rooted in American History, as the tankers 'Memorial Pine Tree.'"

Although the memorial tree was to honor Eisenhower, who lived in Gettysburg, the president could not attend the reunion. He was in Colorado that weekend. However, he placed a notice in the *Gettysburg Times* to his former comrades. It read: "To his Camp Colt comrades: Please extend my warmest greetings to everyone attending the Homecoming Reunion of the World War Tank Corps Association. As you review the experiences gained while you were in active service of your country, you can take added satisfaction from the fact that your Fellow Citizens understand and appreciate the importance of your contributions to the security of our nation. I wish you a most successful and enjoyable reunion."

Less than a month later, the tree was on the verge of dying. On the morning of September 27, Gettysburg National Park Superintendent J. Walter Coleman reported that someone had sawed halfway through the tree's five-inch trunk the night before.

"We'll do everything we can to save it but it's very unlikely that it can survive this damage," he told the newspaper.

The tree was part of a wave of vandalism that hit the park that month. Other damages include smashed wooden signs, damage to a metal historical marker, and a twisted stop sign.

Experts were called in. They trimmed the injured areas and applied preservatives to the tree. They told Coleman "that a tree as large as that, planted as late as August, has only a 50-50 chance of living anyway. And a shock such as it has received reduces its chances considerably," the *Gettysburg Times* reported.

They said they wouldn't know whether the tree had survived until the spring when buds appeared or not.

A few weeks later Bernhard Kolb, foreman of the National Park Service tree repair crew, told the newspaper he was cautiously optimistic about the tree's survival. "If all other things are favorable the tree might come out of it," he said. He added that his crew was making sure that the tree was well watered and that it had the best fertilizer.

The tree managed to survive the damage and remains as a living memorial to Camp Colt and the country's first tank training camp. However, the plaque that commemorates the camp and Eisenhower's command has a typo on it. As pointed out on the website Gettysburg Daily, "Since 1937, the Presidential Inauguration has taken place on January 20th. The marker shows that Eisenhower was inaugurated on January 2, 1953, instead of January 20, 1953. On January 2, 1953,

President-elect Eisenhower was at his residence in New York
City."

The Eisenhower Tree was planted in memory of Camp Colt.
Author's photo.

ODDS & ENDS

Odds & Ends

When Dinosaurs Walked the Battlefield

———————————————

Workers cutting stone at Trostle's Quarry along Bermudian Creek in York Springs didn't think much of the markings on the stones they cut and hauled to the Gettysburg battlefield for bridge construction. Then Elmer R. Hite, an agriculture department engineer with the Highway Engineering and Construction Company, noticed something about the markings.

They were footprints.

Not human footprints, though. Creatures that hadn't walked the earth for millions of years made these footprints.

"Tracks that show claw marks plainly in the outline in the hard sedimentary rock have been uncovered beneath six to 10 feet of solid rock in the quarrying operations," the *Gettysburg Times* reported on July 28, 1937. "Distinctly outlined, fossilized ferns are to be seen on slabs of the stone that bear the imprints of the feet of the huge reptiles."

Workmen hanging off of a 150-foot cliff removed the fossil slabs from the quarry. They were found "in the third and fourth rock strata which lie at an angle of about 60 degrees with the ground surface, indicating that a great upheaval had taken place in that section after the formation of the rock," according to the newspaper.

Because of Hite, the workmen realized that they had

159

made a historic find for the area. However, they also realized that they had probably sent many other similar rocks to be used for bridges.

One of the dinosaur footprints found in the Trostle Quarry in 1937. Photo courtesy of the Adams County Historical Society.

This was a shame because the prints that were found were clear and detailed. They ranged in size from a half-inch to six-inches long. The longest stride between prints was 30 inches. However, over 150 tracks were eventually discovered and saved.

"Most of the footprints are believed to to be those of dinosaurs with three-toe mars plainly showing. In one or two instances the moulds are so clear that the course of blood vessels in the feet and the skin-markings are distinguishable, persons who have seen the prints," the *Gettysburg Times* reported.

Plaster casts were made of the footprints. The best pieces were sent to the Smithsonian Institution for examination. It was hoped that fossilized plants embedded under the footprints would help date the creatures that made the prints. Wave marks on the stone also led scientists to speculate that a large lake was in the area.

Within a week of their discovery, Dr. Arthur B. Cleaves, a state junior geologist, had identified three different creatures from the tracks. They were identified as Anchisauripus exsertus, Anomeopus scambus, and Graliator tennis. Cleaves estimated that these early dinosaurs were only four to six feet in height. The tracks were estimated to be around 175 million years old.

"They had a bird-like type of body, and were not of the heavy type of dinosaur found many years later in the Connecticut valley, the state geologist said," the *Gettysburg Times* reported.

In December 1937, the Smithsonian Institution confirmed that what had been discovered at the quarry was a "dinosaur pasture."

The Smithsonian noted that the dinosaur prints showed that the dinosaurs "seem to have been engaged in leisurely feeding. They often dropped forward so that their front feet were impressed in the mud. Most of the front feet tracks show trace of claws. Their makers were probably flesh-eaters, perhaps grubbing their living from the lake shore ooze. But some show no evidence of claws. They may have been paint browsers, the fore-runners of the herbage-eating dinosaurs who developed into the titans of the race."

Dr. Charles W. Gilmore with the Smithsonian noted that the dinosaurs found in Gettysburg were ancient even when the large dinosaurs that people are more familiar with roamed the earth.

"The creatures were more primitive and generalized than later dinosaurs but were in every respect perfect dinosaurs," Gilmore wrote.

Sharp eyes have also found fossilized prehistoric prints in the stone used in one of the bridges built one the battlefield to span a small creek.

Gettysburg Goes to the World's Fair

 — (decorative divider)

I n 1904, the entire town of Gettysburg went to the St. Louis World's Fair. Not the actual town and its residents but a detailed relief map that depicted over 24 square miles of the town and battlefield.

Engineers with the Gettysburg National Park Commission and under the direction of Emmor Cope, a veteran of the Battle of Gettysburg, created the maps so that "all contours were run by bearings and distances at vertical intervals of 12 feet, all topography obtained by actual surveys by the engineers and no data taken from any other source," according to the *Gettysburg Compiler*.

The commission used Cope's topographic map for its early work to survey land, build roads and build observation towers. Secretary of War Elihu Root authorized the project and it included all the area's buildings, roads and avenues. The final scale of the map was 1:200 horizontally and 1:72 vertically and showed 24.15 square miles. The dimensions were 9' 3" by 12' 8".

"It is composed of successive layers of white pine strips 1/8 inch thick, out to the shapes of the corresponding contours on the topographical map, glued and pegged together," the *Compiler* reported. Each layer of wood represented 12 feet of height and each layer was applied so that the wood grain ran perpendicular to the layers it was between. The sharp edges were then shaved to smooth out the contours.

The entire project took more than a year to create with the actual construction of the map taking about nine months.

"The map shows practically everything on the surface of the ground, all streams, runs, ditches and the like the division of land into fields appears, the kind of fence, whether post or rail, tapeworm, or stone, is made plain on the map; so much of the ground is covered brush, or timber is made plain. The farm buildings are all accurately located. Gettysburg on the map is a perfect miniature. The shape of the houses is preserved. Any building can be instantly recognized," the *Compiler* reported.

In 1904, this wooden relief map of the Gettysburg battlefield was first displayed at the St. Louis World's Fair. Courtesy of *GettysburgDaily.com.*

Before heading off for display in St. Louis, the relief map was placed on exhibition at the Winter Building in town on April 5 and 6 so that anyone who wanted to see the map could do so.

The 1904 World's Fair ran from April 30, 1904, to December 1, 1904. It planned celebrate the 1803 Louisiana Purchase, but the opening was delayed to allow greater international participation (62 foreign counties took part). The fair covered 1,200 acres in St. Louis and had more than 1,500 buildings connected by 75 miles of roads and walkways. During its run, 19.7 million people visited the fair.

While at the World's Fair, the relief was on display at the Battle Abbey building that opened on June 1. Admission was 25 cents for adults and 15 cents for children. Once in the building, they could view the map and other things like:

A recreated medieval castle (400 feet x 250 feet) complete with towers, bastions, parapet and drawbridge.

A battle history and war museum of the American Republic with guides dressed historic American military uniforms.

Six plastic cycloramas that showed the battles of Yorktown (Revolutionary War, 1781), New Orleans (War of 1812), Buena Vista (Mexican War, 1846), Manassas and Gettysburg (Civil War, 1861/1863), Custer's Massacre (last stand, 1876), Manila (Spanish-American War, 1898).

After the fair closed, another wooden map was created so that one copy could be kept in Washington, D.C. and the other copy kept in Gettysburg. According to *GettysburgDaily.com*, the Gettysburg copy was kept in the county office building (the current Adams County Public Library). It was then moved to the old cyclorama building and it is now on display in the Gettysburg National Military Park Visitor's Center.

Medal of Honor
Purchased for a Dime

H ugh Krebs of Chambersburg was a collector so it seemed only natural he would become an antiques dealer. He prowled yard sales, flea markets and estate auctions looking for trinkets and treasures that caught his eye.

In 1946, Krebs was "nosing through items," as he put it, which were offered for sale at an auction in Adams County. A box of loose and small items had been set aside because nobody had been interested in them. It was a "junk" box, according to the *Chambersburg Public Opinion*. However, it was also selling for only a dime.

Since he was a general collector and not searching for anything in particular, Krebs rooted through the box to see if it was even worth a dime. Inside, he found a piece of history. It was a 19th Century Congressional Medal of Honor.

Krebs soon found out that even among Congressional Medals of Honor, the one he had found stood alone. "A Congressional Medal of Honor, the only one awarded to a soldier who disobeyed orders in a time of war, ends up in a box of worthless trinkets and junk to be sold for ten cents," Pete Ritter wrote in the *Public Opinion*.

The Medal of Honor that Krebs had purchased for 10 cents had been bought through the preservation of soldiers' lives and a Union artillery line during the Battle of Gettysburg.

On the third day of the battle, Capt. William E. Miller

from Carlisle commanded four companies of the 3rd Pennsylvania Cavalry. He was sick and barely able to sit in his saddle, but he hoped that he and his men wouldn't be engaged in any fighting that day. Miller's commander had ordered him to hold his position in the woods along Low Dutch Road, southeast of Gettysburg, under any conditions.

Medal of Honor Winner
William E. Miller

From his position, Miller watched as Confederate cavalry assembled into eight regiments. He could also see what was drawing them together. The Confederate cavalrymen would try to break through the Union line to destroy the artillery pieces that were pounding their fellow soldiers engaged in Pickett's Charge.

It was possible they would succeed. The Confederate cavalry outnumbered the Michigan cavalry, which were the only defenders between them and the Union artillery.

"The Michigan cavalry mustered to charge the onrushing sabres of the Confederate horsemen when Capt. Miller, seeing the obvious strategy, turned to his first lieutenant, William Rhawl Brook, asking his support in disobeying the order to hold fast at that point. Brook agreed," Ritter wrote.

Miller led the charge of the 3rd Pennsylvania. The Confederate cavalry focused on the Michigan cavalry and didn't see the charge on their flank until it was too late. The 3rd Pennsylvania split the Confederate line, disrupting the Confederate charge. Rather than a penetrating charge through the Union line, the Confederate cavalrymen found themselves engaged in close quarters sabre battles.

Miller was wounded in the battle with what he laughed off as "a little hole in the arm." Though the official records did not mention his role in the action, it was not forgotten. "In July 1897, the Congressional Medal of Honor was bestowed upon Capt. Miller by President McKinley and presented by Secretary of War Russell A. Alger, who as a colonel in the 5th Michigan Cavalry witnessed the battle," Ritter wrote.

Miller died in 1919 and is buried in National Cemetery in Gettysburg.

How the medal came to be in a junk box sold at auction is not known. Krebs sought out any descendants of Miller's but found no one.

Once it became known Krebs had the medal, different historical societies and the Carlisle American Legion made offers to buy it from him. He turned them all down. Once Krebs learned the story behind the medal, he knew it was worth over 10 cents. It was priceless.

The First Battle of Gettysburg

W hile the 1863 clash between North and South made Gettysburg famous, the original Battle of Gettysburg probably took place thousands of years earlier.

The history of white men in this area date back a few hundred years, but archaeologists found evidence of Paleo-Indians in this area beginning in 1926. Paleo-Indians were nomadic hunter-gatherers who did not plant crops or form permanent settlements.

"The Paleoindian Period in North America begins around 16,000 years ago when humans first entered into the New World at the close of the last Ice Age and ends around 10,000 years ago when the climate began to warm quickly," according to Penn State Public Broadcasting.

After the glaciers from the Ice Age retreated from this area, grassland and conifer forests grew up to cover the land. More than 300 sites have been found in Pennsylvania that show evidence of Paleo-Indians. Nearly all of them are found along major rivers in the state. Although this sounds like a lot, Pennsylvania has an inventory of more than 22,000 archeological sites from all time periods.

"Travel was probably easier along the flat river valleys and although there is no evidence for canoes, there is a strong probability they were used," according to Penn State Public Broadcasting. "It is assumed that these people traveled along the same river valleys each year, searching for the necessary resources. This annual pattern of movements is called their seasonal round."

Fluted points were first found in this area in 1926. "Until then archaeologists did not know for sure if life existed here 10,000 or more years ago," according to the *Gettysburg Times*.

Early archaic chipped spear points. Photo courtesy of the Pennsylvania Historical and Museum Commission

Fluted points are unique to this side of the world. They are spear points with a channel along each face of the blade made by striking a flake from the base. The oldest type are called Clovis points. The flute is believed to have made it easier to attach the point to a wooden or bone shaft to become a thrusting spear. "Imagine killing a mammoth or a bison with a bayonet! In the west where Pleistocene megafauna bones are more frequently preserved because of current drier conditions, fluted points have been found at 'kill sites' where they are mixed with the bones of mammoth, mastodon, horse, camel, bison and peccary," according to Penn State Public Broadcasting.

Back then, the Adams County area was apparently a "tourist" destination. It had no permanent human population. It was a "no man's land" between the Potomac and Susquehanna rivers, State Anthropologist John Witthoft, told the Adams County Historical Society in 1952. He said the area was "a mecca for Indian tribes from the lower Potomac and from as far north as the Finger Lakes section of New York. They came here for rhyolite and other native stone to use in making spear and arrow heads and other stone tools upon which the Indians depended."

Rhyolite is a volcanic rock that often appears glassy. Adams County once had one America's leading rhyolite quarries at Carbaugh Run.

As a unique place to find this stone, the area was a destination site, even in prehistoric days.

Witthoft "indicated that the first battle here between Northerners and Southerners probably did not take place in 1863 but 10,000 years before when New York and Maryland and Virginia Indians clashed here on trips to get 'armaments'," the *Gettysburg Times* reported.

Although there are stories of the Indians who roamed this region during the same time as white men settling the area, "Most Indian relics found in this area do not date from American colonial days but are from 5,000 to 10,000 years old," according to the *Gettysburg Times*. In fact, the newspaper notes that little evidence of Indians in this area from 1,500 B.C. to establishment of white settlements exists, and there is no sign of permanent Indian settlements.

The Paleo-Indians eventually gave way to the Early Archaic Indians. This transition was marked by the end of the use of fluted points that happened around 10,000 years ago. Vegetation changed as more spruce and pine forests grew.

The Second
Battle of Gettysburg Begins

I n 2005, the U.S. Supreme Court decided in the case of Kelo v. City of New London that government could use eminent domain not just to claim property for the public good but to actually take it from one private owner and give it to another private owner for the public good. In the Kelo case, the government took property from its owner and gave it to a private developer on the promise of redevelopment benefits to the community.

You may wonder what this has to do with Gettysburg history. Well, if wasn't for the time that Gettysburg had a case before the Supreme Court, the court may have decided the Kelo case differently.

The Gettysburg Electric Railway was incorporated in July 1892. The trolley system was planned to not only carry people throughout Gettysburg but to also take tourists out onto the battlefield. A Philadelphia newspaper reported that the route "will start from the square in Gettysburg, run out the Baltimore Pike, pass Cemetery Hill, encircle the National Cemetery, thence along the Emmittsburg Rd. to the Peach Orchard, through the Wheatfield to Devil's Den, and through the Valley of Death to Little Round Top Park. The return will be made via the Bloody Angle and Hancock Avenue to Gettysburg."

As part of the construction, a group of Italian workmen

from Baltimore blasted on William Tipton's land that contained Devil's Den. The explosions were loud enough people in Gettysburg heard them.

One eyewitness wrote, "All along the line, in the vicinity of Devil's Den, there is heavy blasting and digging and filling; and great havoc is played with the landscape. Huge masses of rock are displaced, great boulders are moved, the valley is to be filled the width and height of a track from the bridge over Plum Run in front of Round Top to the north end of the Valley and a whole new appearance will be given to the famous field of carnage," according to Nancy Householder on the Gettysburg Discussion Group .

As the 30-foot-wide path was cut through the historic site, veterans and some citizens grew more and more worried that a national landmark would be lost.

"Historic trees were felled, streams were forded, and rocks that still show the scars of battle were forever blasted from the face of the earth. In some instances the trolley roadbed passed within feet of monuments that had been dedicated just a few years before. Public outcry was immediate and in some cases very bitter," Householder wrote.

John Bachelder came to Gettysburg in June 1893 to see the situation first hand and make a preliminary report to the U.S. Secretary of War. He wrote, in part, "The boulders which covered the combatants in the desperate engagement between the 4th Maine and the 44th New York of the Union Army and the 44th Alabama and the right of Bennings Brigade of the Confederate army are already blasted, and the fragments broken under the hammer and are covered with earth to form a roadbed. And it is this locality which has been turned into a park to which cheap excursions are to be run from Baltimore and other cities. This is the most wild and picturesque section of the field. For the distance of over one mile before reaching this locality, the road cuts ruthlessly through the scene of some of the most desperate encounters of the battle."

Though the opponents to the trolley could do little to stop construction because the track was being laid on private lands, that benefit soon turned against the Gettysburg Electric Railway and brought progress to halt. The 72nd Pennsylvania Infantry Regiment owned a tract of land at The Angle that the railway needed to cross. The regiment refused to grant the railway a right of way. Because of this, the Gettysburg Electric Railway Company was forced to use a portion of the Gettysburg and Harrisburg Railroad to run along the Emmitsburg Road.

And so began the second Battle of Gettysburg.

The Gettysburg Trolley running near Devil's Den. Courtesy of the Adams County Historical Society.

Government Takings

"The idea of the Nation acquiring an entire battlefield and preserving it for historical purposes was new in 1890. It is therefore not surprising that it soon engendered a serious controversy, which arose, fittingly enough, at Gettysburg," Ronald F. Lee wrote in *The origins & evolution of the national park idea.*

Tensions between supporters and opponents of the Gettysburg Trolley rose with each explosion and felled tree. In 1893, 40 people asked the Pennsylvania Attorney General to step in and stop the trolley, but 326 people signed a petition in favor of the trolley.

Attorney General William Hensel refused to step in. He wrote, in part, "the right of owners of private property—whatever public interest may attach to it—to dispose of it to passenger railway corporations, cannot be disputed. ...the line itself...has been chosen with a view of affording tourists the best possible means of visiting and viewing this great battlefield and doing the least possible injury to its natural conditions."

While trolley line construction halted in August 1893 because of a lack of funds, operations began in September as far as the tracks ran at that point. However, the company was insolvent and went into receivership. The trolley continued operating, though, and track laying continued as revenue came in. By 1895, the trolley had 8.5 miles of track.

In 1894, Congress adopted a joint resolution specifically use the power of government to stop the private company. The resolution noted that was "imminent danger that portions of said battlefield may be irreparably defaced by the construction of a railway over same" and it gave the Secretary of War the ability to acquire the land by purchase or condemnation.

The Gettysburg Railway Company refused to sell and the government began condemnation proceedings in June

1894. The trolley sued the government to stop the eminent domain action. The United States Circuit Court sided with the trolley company. Judge George Dallas noted in his decision that the "powers of congress are distinctly enumerated in the constitution, and in that enumeration none is included to which the uses for which it is proposed to condemn this land can be related, without, in my opinion, enlarging the constitutional grant by grafting upon its express terms a construction so lax and comprehensive as to be subversive of its limited character."

Gettysburg trolley running through town. Courtesy of the Adams County Historical Society.

On November 3, 1894, the jury identified $30,000 "as the measure of damage that would be done the Trolley by the proposed change". Both the government and trolley company appealed the ruling because the amount with either too low (trolley company) or too high (federal government).

"When the court eventually handed down an award of $30,000, attorneys for the company rejected the finding and filed exceptions, claiming that establishment of Gettysburg National Park was not a public purpose within the meaning of earlier legislation and that 'preserving lines of battle' and properly marking with tablets the positions occupied" were not public uses which permitted the condemnation of private property by the United States. The case finally went before the highest court in the Nation," Lee wrote.

The trolley company agreed on Nov. 12 to move its route from near Devil's Den if the government paid its expenses. The government refused. Also, the federal government started condemnation on another tract of land in January 1895, which was also denied in circuit court.

The case went to the U.S. Supreme Court, which unanimously ruled in 1896 in favor of the federal government. Justice Rufus Peckham wrote in the decision, "Can it be that the government is without power to preserve the land and properly mark out the various sites upon which this struggle took place? Can it not erect the monuments provided for by these acts of Congress, or even take possession of the field of battle in the name and for the benefit of all the citizens of the country for the present and for the future? Such a use seems necessarily not only a public use, but one so closely connected with the welfare of the republic itself as to be within the powers granted Congress by the Constitution for the purpose of protecting and preserving the whole country. It would be a great object lesson to all who looked upon the land thus cared for, and it would show a proper recognition of the great things that were done there on those momentous days. By this use, the government manifests for the benefit of all its citizens the value put upon the services and exertions of the citizen soldiers of that period."

The decision reversed the lower court rulings in favor of the Gettysburg Electric Railway and allowed the federal government to force the trolley company to move its route.

Lee wrote that the decision "established the principle that battlefield preservation was a public use for which the US government's Constitutional power of eminent domain could be used."

The trolley continued to operate in Gettysburg until November 1916 along a different route.

However, the United States v. Gettysburg Electric Railway Company case was part of case law, and it has had modern impact. It is often cited as justification for the actions taken in the Kelo v. City of New London where the city took private property from one person to give to another private entity.

Out-of-this-World Tourists on the Gettysburg Battlefield

On July 7, 1947, a group of Gettysburg College students was enjoying a picnic on the Gettysburg battlefield near the Pennsylvania monument when they saw tourists who came from way, way, out of town.

Around 3:30 p.m., the group saw five or six discs that were gray and shiny in appearance dart eastward across the sky. A few minutes later, the discs returned and did the same thing again.

"Each time, they were traveling in two distinct groups," said Frank Toms, a Gettysburg College senior. "I should say they were six inches in diameter and about 150 to 200 feet above the ground."

Gettysburg had joined the ranks of many other communities across the country where residents had reported seeing flying saucers. The problem with the Gettysburg report is that it most likely was a hoax.

The day after the report was made a Philadelphia newspaper pointed out that "Park officials here said today they knew of no picnic held in the rain Monday afternoon on the battlefield," according to the *Gettysburg Times*.

Since all of the witnesses were members of the Sigma Chi fraternity, *The (Hanover) Evening Sun* called the fraternity house and was told that there had been an outing on the afternoon in question. When the reporter asked to talk to any of the witnesses, he was told that none of them were there at the time. The Philadelphia newspaper also got a similar obfuscation with the fraternity unwilling to confirm or deny the UFO sighting.

However, it seems unlikely that there had been a picnic on the battlefield on the afternoon in question if it had been raining.

What seems more likely is that the members of the Sigma Chi fraternity read the article in the *Gettysburg Times* that ran the day of the picnic titled, "More Flying Saucers are Puzzling U.S." The article noted, "From one end of the country to the other, new reports of disk-like 'flying saucers' skimming through the skies today added to the mystery which has baffled the nation since June 25."

The sightings had started in Washington State on June 25 and spread through the western states. Sightings had peaked over the July 4th weekend when the first sighting east of the Mississippi River had been reported. By the time of the Gettysburg sighting, reports of flying saucers had been made in 38 states, Washington D.C., and Canada in a span of two weeks.

Not all of the reports described the same objects and the objects didn't always move in the same way. For instance, Mrs. A. C. Smith of Towanda, Pa., reported that she had seen two flying saucers hovering 20 feet above her house and that they had "bobbed about, merged together, separated and disappeared," according to the *Gettysburg Times*. Other reports varied the size of the flying saucers and some said the flying saucers made various sounds.

Throughout all of this, the Army, Navy, Atomic Energy Commission, and Air Force were all denying any knowledge about what the flying saucers were or if they were even real.

With the Gettysburg report debunked, the reports also warned that Pennsylvania state law provided a penalty for anyone giving false information to a newspaper. However, nothing could be found to say whether that penalty was ever applied against the fraternity.

In response to the great number of UFO reports, the Air Force started Project Blue Book in 1952. It ran until the end of 1969, at which time, it had collected 12,618 reports. The purpose of the study was to determine whether UFOs were a national security threat and to scientifically analyze the reports.

A search of the records shows that the Gettysburg area had one reported UFO sighting in Project Blue Book. This one happened in 1952 near Zora. Three people saw a large, circular, white object high in the sky. According to the report, it was "drifting very fast towards the northwest."

At the conclusion of Project Blue Book, one finding was that most of the UFO reports were misidentified natural phenomena or conventional aircraft.

Where Fairytales Came to Life

I t was a place a place where happy family memories were made, and now it only exists as happy family memories. Fantasyland entertained tens of thousands of youngsters and the young at heart from 1959 to 1980.

Kenneth and Thelma Dick took their family to the shore for a vacation in 1957. On their way home, they stopped at Storybook Land near Atlantic City, N.J. It was a small park, planned to entertain young children like the three Dick girls.

"My mother kept saying the whole time, 'I could do better than this. This is so okay, but I could do something so cute,'" Jaqueline White said. She is the middle child of the three Dick girls between her sisters, Stephanie and Cynthia.

White's parents spent the four hours of the drive home, planning the park and how they would market it. Because they wanted to locate it where there were a lot of people, the Dicks had decide on whether they would build their park in Lancaster or Gettysburg.

Gettysburg won, in part because Kenneth Dick was from this area and was a graduate of Biglerville High School. However, the Dicks also had a strategic reason for locating the Fantasyland in Gettysburg.

"Parents bring their children to Gettysburg, and they will climb on the cannons and run across the field, but after an hour, they'll be saying, 'Dad, what else is there to do?' Fantasyland gave little kids something to do," White said.

Fantasyland 1863 opened in July 1959. "This is Fantasyland...," the brochure promised. "a world set apart...a world where stories...and dreams...of elves and fairies...and all the storybook characters come to life...in a beautiful setting with the 'gentle look' of long ago."

Fantasyland was a theme park located on a portion of the Gettysburg Battlefield. Photo courtesy of Jaqueline White.

To enter the park, you walked through a short door that part of a large storybook. The door was only five feet tall. If a person walked in without stooping, he or she was charged the children's price of 60 cents. People who stooped paid the adult admission of a dollar.

"We had a lot of grandmothers get in for the children's price," White said. "They loved it."

The first thing a person saw walking into the park was a 23-foot-tall Mother Goose statue with her goose. A girl in the storybook office could see visitors approaching the statue and speak to them through a microphone, so it sounded like Mother Goose was speaking to visitors. It delighted the younger children. Children could also talk to several different live costumed characters, such as Raggedy Ann and Andy, Little Bo Beep, the Easter Bunny, or a Fairy Princess.

Mother Goose greeted visitors as they entered the park. Photo courtesy of Jaqueline White.

The park was originally 23 acres, but grew over time to 35 acres as new attractions were added. While most of the attractions had a storybook character theme like the Old Woman Who Lived in a Shoe or Rapunzel's Castle, you could also visit Santa's Village, watch a Wild West Show, take in an animal show where rabbits and chickens had been trained to play baseball, basketball, and the piano. The park featured 11 rides, four live shows, and several displays.

"The Winter Wonderland started out as a scary inside ride, but we bought it, and my mother transformed it into the Winter Wonderland," White said.

Thelma had a gift for things like that. She created beautiful gardens throughout the park and designed many of the attractions. On a Christmas trip to New York City, she enjoyed the window displays in Macy's so much that she walked into the store and bought all of the displays. She then had buildings constructed with each one holding a moving Christmas display. This became Santa's Village. Musselman's even paid for apple-oriented attraction to be constructed at the park.

"I liked it best at night," White said. "We stayed open until 10 p.m. and we had the trees full of colored lights that we turned on. It was beautiful."

This was all amid a wooded setting with trails that wound through landscaped gardens. You could also see plenty of live animals, such as tame fawns, trained rabbits, calves, and raccoons.

Fantasyland was immediate hit. *The Gettysburg Times* noted in 1959, "'Fantasyland,' which is Gettysburg's newest major tourist attraction, outgrew its facilities for handling crowds on the second day of its operation." During the opening weekend, 4,500 people entered the park and that number grew to 4,800 by the third weekend. Weekdays saw 500 to

700 people a day visiting the park.

"We never turned anybody away," White said.

A second entrance even had to be built to handle the weekend crowds.

White started working at the park when she was only eight years old. She played Little Red Riding Hood walking through the park and talking to the visitors. As she got older, she performed other duties. Even once she was married and working as a teacher, White and her husband still worked summers at the park.

"My husband, John, went to Dickinson Law School and worked at the park in the summer. I taught at Cumberland Valley High School and in summers worked at the park," White said.

White's sisters, Stephanie and Cythia, also grew up working in Fantasyland doing a variety of jobs.

"My oldest sister was mentally retarded and my parents always said that part of their reason for doing Fantasyland was to give her something to do," White said. "She loved it there. She was down there all of the time."

The park was also the first job that many people in the area had since they could work there as young as 14. During the season, the Dicks used three dozen people at the park. Throughout the life of the park, White says there were more than 200 different employees.

"I still get people coming up to me and saying that working at Fantasyland was their first job," White said.

The park even had the distinction of being visited by First Lady Jacqueline Kennedy and her children, Caroline and John John, a couple times.

"The youngsters both had special things they wished to show their mother and sometimes, like most mothers with two small children, Mrs. Kennedy found herself being tugged in two different directions at once."

President Eisenhower's grandchildren also enjoyed visiting the park from time to time. In fact, Eisenhower's granddaughter, Ann Eisenhower, worked at the park.

One attraction in Fantasyland. Photo courtesy of Jaqueline White.

"Ann was Mother Goose when Jackie Kennedy came," White said. "She talked to the kids and then ran down the stairs because one of the Secret Service men had been her Secret Service man, and she wanted to say, 'Hi.'"

Not everything went smoothly at the park, though. Once the sky ride started making a funny noise, so the operator hit the emergency button and the ride halted with people still on it. The fire department had to come in with ladder trucks to get the stranded riders down.

The popular train ride in Fantasyland. Photo courtesy of Jaqueline White.

White remembers another time when the squirrel monkeys and chimpanzees got loose from the live animal show.

"They ended up in Colt Park," White said. "I remember the police running around trying to catch them. It was funny. I don't remember how they did it, but they did finally trap all of them."

The park also had its detractors who claimed Fantasyland

represented the over-commercialization of Gettysburg. During its first year in operation, the entrance to the park was opposite Meade's Headquarters. Some editorials were written opposing the park's location, but nothing could be done about it.

Then in 1974, the National Park Service bought the property, but allowed the park another 10 years of operation. White said the money was too much for her parents, who had grown up poor, to pass up.

Once the park was sold, the Dicks advertised through trade associations that the equipment and shows were for sale. Sports Paradise in New Concord, Ohio, purchased everything. The park's final season was 1980.

"They came in and cut the buildings apart, loaded everything on trucks and hauled it away," White said.

You can still find some of the remnants of Fantasyland at other parks around the country. The carousel is at a park in Austin, Texas, and Mother Goose is at Storybook Land in New Jersey.

"I still go there sometimes just to see her," White said. "They [the park owners] told me that people have come there and see her and recognize her as being from Fantasyland."

Signs of the park locally are long gone and the Gettysburg National Military Park Visitor's Center now occupies land that was once part of Fantasyland, but there are still plenty of people in Gettysburg who remember when fairy tale characters used to live in the woods.

Acknowledgments

I wanted to thank all of those people who helped me put the *Secrets of the Gettysburg Battlefield* together. The longer I work as a writer, the more I realize that while one person may publish a book, the effort is much richer when others assist.

To that end, I'd like to thank the Adams County Historical Society and the volunteers there. They were generous with their time when I had questions, and they allowed me to use some of his pictures in this book. They also were available to answer questions I might have throughout the process.

I'd also like to thank Alex Hayes, editor of the *Gettysburg Times,* and Krista Scarlett, editor of *Celebrate Gettysburg*. Both have been willing to publish my history articles over the years.

Finally, I'd like to thank Grace Eyler for not only another great-looking cover but also being able to create the template for the Secrets series.

I have probably missed someone who I'll remember after this book goes to print. If so, it's not because I didn't appreciate your input. I sometimes get confused juggling all of the projects I do. If I left you out, mention it to me.

In putting together *Secrets of the Gettysburg Battlefield*, I have enjoyed looking beyond the stories of the Civil War that dominate the town where I live. I could find unique stories that took place on the battlefield. Some were Civil War stories. That's hard to avoid when writing about a battlefield. It's also hard to find something different about the Battle of Gettysburg that hasn't been written about dozens of times before.

Others stories just happened to take place the same place as the largest battle of the Civil War. I just needed to come across them while I was researching.

The result is a book I hope you enjoy.

James Rada, Jr.
January 30, 2017

About the Author

J ames Rada, Jr. has written many works of historical fiction and non-fiction history. They include the popular books *Saving Shallmar: Christmas Spirit in a Coal Town, Canawlers,* and *Battlefield Angels: The Daughters of Charity Work as Civil War Nurses.*

He lives in Gettysburg, Pa., where he works as a free-lance writer. James has received numerous awards from the Maryland-Delaware-DC Press Association, Associated Press, Maryland State Teachers Association, Society of Professional Journalists, and Community Newspapers Holdings, Inc. for his newspaper writing.

If you would like to keep up to date on new books James publishes or ask him questions, you can e-mail him at *jimrada@yahoo.com.*

To see James' other books or to order copies online, go to *www.jamesrada.com.*

PLEASE LEAVE A REVIEW

If you enjoyed this book, please help other readers find it. Reviews help the author get more exposure for his books. Please take a few minutes to review this book at *Amazon.com* or *Goodreads.com*. Thank you, and if you sign up for my mailing list at *jamesrada.com*, you can get FREE ebooks.

Don't Miss These Books By James Rada, Jr.

Secrets of Garrett County: Little-Known Stories & Hidden History from Maryland's Westernmost County

Known for its natural beauty, Garrett County is made up of interesting people, places, and events that make it unique. From the time the CIA poisoned people with LSD at Deep Creek Lake to the story of the Black Widow Murderess of Grantsville, these stories will intrigue you. *Secrets of Garrett County* includes 44 fascinating stories and 58 pictures.

Secrets of the C&O Canal: Little-Known Stories & Hidden History Along the Potomac River

The 184.5-mile-long C&O Canal runs along the Maryland side of the Potomac River. From its connections with the U.S. Constitution to the JFK assassination, the canal has lots of stories that even many canal enthusiasts don't know. These are stories of floods, murders, war, and tragedy. *Secrets of the C&O Canal* includes 30 stories and 67 illustrations and photos.

Available wherever books are sold.

Made in the USA
Middletown, DE
09 August 2021